PRAISE FOR URBAN PANTRY

"As someone who loves cookbooks (I used to take them to bed and read them like you would a novel) and is primarily self taught from the old greats, I still derive plenty of inspiration from the books that come out every year. Here are some of the standouts that I will be delving into all summer. Among them is Amy Pennington's book Urban Pantry, *full of clever recipes for using your kitchen to the max...[She] incorporates many tips on how to grow your own kitchen garden and teaches a kitchen economy for today's urbanite—from how to stock the pantry, to what to plant when, to how to can and preserve a variety of foods for the winter months."*

– Gwyneth Paltrow, *Goop Newsletter*, goop.com

"A tasty collection of seasonal and sustainable recipes that can be prepared using staples pulled from the cupboard."

– Leslie Kelly, *Al Dente*, www.aldenteblog.com

"A must read!"

– Urban Farm Hub, www.urbanfarmhub.com

"Pennington offers up pithy advice on kitchen economy and stocking a practical pantry. Her recipes, from soups to pickles to temptations like vanilla quinoa pudding, offer ease of preparation and healthful ingredients. But gardeners will cruise through the recipes to savor the chapter called "The Pantry Garden" on how to choose and grow flavorful herbs and vegetables to cook and eat fresh from the garden, as well as to preserve for the pantry."

– Valerie Easton, *Pacific Northwest Magazine*, The Seattle Times

urban pantry

Tips & Recipes
for a Thrifty, Sustainable
& Seasonal Kitchen

AMY PENNINGTON

PHOTOGRAPHY BY DELLA CHEN

SKIPSTONE

Published by Skipstone, an imprint of
The Mountaineers Books
Printed in the United States of America

13 12 11 10   5 4 3

Copy Editor: Amy Smith Bell
Design: Jane Jeszeck/Jigsaw, www.jigsawseattle.com
Cover photograph: Della Chen

ISBN (paperback): 978-1-59485-346-3
ISBN (ebook): 978-1-59485-347-0

Library of Congress Cataloging-in-Publication Data

Pennington, Amy, 1974-
  Urban pantry : tips and recipes for a thrifty, sustainable
& seasonal kitchen / by Amy Pennington ; photography
by Della Chen.
      p. cm.
  Includes index.
  ISBN 978-1-59485-346-3
  1. Cookery. I. Title.
  TX714.P4455 2010
  641.5—dc22
                            2009049748

♺ Printed on recycled paper

Skipstone books may be purchased for corporate, educational, or other promotional sales. For special discounts and information, contact our Sales Department at 800-553-4453 or mbooks@mountaineersbooks.org.

Skipstone
1001 SW Klickitat Way
Suite 201
Seattle, Washington 98134
206.223.6303
www.skipstonebooks.org
www.mountaineersbooks.org

LIVE LIFE. MAKE RIPPLES.

To all of the children I love so very much:
Lily Zimmerman and Daniel Abramson; Seth Pennington IV;
Michael, Lauren, Katarina, Jaclyn, and Nathalie Bartholomew;
Hannah Maloy-Collado; and Lilly, Caleb, and Luke Ackerman.
May you be playful in life, confident in the kitchen, and surrounded
by friends and good food, always.

CONTENTS

LIST OF RECIPES

acknowledgments

I WOULD LIKE to give a shout-out to the best collaborator *ever* who brought life to the pages of this, my very first book—photographer Della Chen. Her humor, dedication, and overall Gemini fabulousness is so very appreciated. I owe her a lifetime of free gardening advice.

Big props to the team over at Skipstone who found me out in the garden and followed me into the kitchen, where my heart and soul live—Kate Rogers, Margaret Sullivan, and team.

A thank-you to top all thank-yous to my very best friends and urban family who have spent countless hours around the stove and dinner table with me—Michelle Ackerman, Marcus White, Jaime Collado, and Patric Gabre-Kidan. I love you all dearly.

A gracious thank-you to Miss Ritzy Ryziak for giving me my first writing job (offered to me in the doorway of a pizzeria) before I even knew I wanted to be a food writer.

I am forever indebted to Tom Douglas for opening the door to a wonderful world of food, and sharing his experiences, wisdom, words, and support, *always*.

A big thank-you to all of my clever food friends for their inspired and creative suggestions, cooking tips, eager ears, and hours of conversation about nothing but food—John Chaffetz, Sheri Wetherell, Barnaby Dorfman, and Katie Okumura. And to my good-food girls—Jen Lamson, Kristin Hyde, and Emily Naftlin—for being my tasting guinea pigs and offering me their candid thoughts on everything food related.

I am beyond grateful to all of the people who have given me so much inspiration over the years—in life and in food. I think of them often and fondly and continue to use their tricks in the kitchen and beyond—Carol Zimmerman, Lynda Oosterhuis, and Aliye Aydin.

And finally, *Puno hvala mojoj obitelji!*

Volim te, Gram! Thanks to my sister and brother, who continue to pepper my life with good stories and laughter; to my mother, who let me cook by myself when I was too short to even see the top of the stove; and to my father, who taught me that the phrase "I can't" should forever be banished from my lexicon and raised me to be the self-sustaining woman I am today.

preface

A FEW YEARS BACK, I found myself in a good friend's kitchen playing maestro over multiple pots and pans in chorus on the stovetop for our weekly Sunday Family Dinner. One pot had water set to boil, another contained olive oil and butter at the ready. I had the oven preheating, and various bowls and spoons, cutting boards and dish towels were strewn about the kitchen. A typical night, with me hovered over a hot stove, red-faced with glistening brow, while I half-listened to the chatter coming from the other room. I was in heaven. Until I went sleuthing for some ingredients. "Marcus!" I hollered, crouching inside his small pantry closet. "Where's the flour?" Scurrying from his host duties, Marcus peered over my shoulder quizzically.

The interesting thing about dinner at Marcus's apartment is that Marcus seldom cooks. Anything. I'm not sure how he's managed to surround himself with a bunch of food-loving friends, but that's exactly what he's done. To name just a few of us: Jimmy is a caterer, Rusty has cooked in Marrakech, Patric is a trained pastry chef, Lynda has worked in kitchens for years. And because we all love food and enjoy cooking, Marcus inevitably holds court in the other room. His pantry was, in a word, dismal. My requests for such simple items as butter were met with a sheepish grin. There is no whipping up of meals at Marcus's house. You need to have a plan if you're going to cook in his kitchen. Usually we all show up with canvas bags packed full of ingredients, unpack them to cook, and then pack up what's left over at the end of the night.

Eventually, I started hauling over random jars and containers of pantry items, filling Marcus's cupboards on my own. I have single-handedly stocked his pantry with powdered sugar, cornstarch, shortening, olive oil, wheat flour, kasha, parsley, lemons, limes, and more. I don't mind making do with missing ingredients on occasion, but as I began to cook more often in his apartment, I wanted more ingredients on hand. The good news is that Marcus started stocking his pantry as well, and these days I'll show up to him proudly holding out a new item. Another interesting thing happened over the years—Marcus actually started to cook. And experiment. And play in his very own kitchen. These days, he is actually quite a good cook. Sure, he calls for advice as he stands in the aisles of a grocery store pondering which cut of meat to get, but I get those calls all the time from other friends. It's like I'm the 911 lifeline of food. I can't take all the credit for shaping Marcus's culinary adventures, but it has been interesting (and delicious) to take part in his pantry progression.

This is a book about stocking your pantry. Not just any old pantry, but an urbanite's pantry full of new and interesting ingredients that come together quickly and inexpensively and turn out stellar, inspired meals—all while focusing on eco-fabulous techniques and ingredients. When I write it all down like that, the idea seems pretty lofty, but it's actually completely practical. Simply put: It's nice to have fancy things around the kitchen. It feels good to peer into a cupboard and see jars of beans and grains and jams. Feels like home.

I'm a city girl who grew up in the country. My parents moved out to Long Island from Brooklyn and Queens so that they could live the "simple life." My dad had this thing about livin' off the land. We kept chickens and ducks, collected fresh eggs, raised a pig for its bacon, and kept a few goats for milk and cream. We also kept a vegetable garden out back, and come spring I would sneak snap peas off the vine, thinking I'd get in trouble if I got caught eating one. I learned to squeeze the pod between my fingers and decide which would offer the sweetest peas. Too big and they lost their flavor, too small and I felt cheated. As kids, we ate berries from the bushes, sipped pollen from the flutes of honeysuckle blossoms, and in general tried to get our snacks off the land.

What we couldn't get from our yard in Long Island, we hunted, fished, and foraged for. I grew up on the water and had my own fishing pole before I was in school. My sister and brother and I would sit for hours on Peconic Lake, catching small sunfish or trout to fry up and an occasional turtle, which we never could figure out how to eat. Scaling and gutting a fish was second nature. During crab season we would wake up just before the crack of dawn (with the rooster) and pack up our tackle boxes, rods, and nets for daylong crabbing adventures. My parents never worried about us falling into the Great South Bay, where we dropped crab nets and cast our lines. "Better swim, I guess," my father would say as we keened our bodies out over the edge of docks and shorelines. I learned how to set traps, which bait was best to use, and how not to cast my shadow on the water. We'd come home from crabbing, dirty and sun-kissed, and steam the crabs in big pots until the house smelled of sea. I learned to associate the damp morning salt air with the taste of steamed crabs. I didn't realize I was learning that smells and tastes make keen memories, of course. It just sort of happened.

The country-bumpkin vibe stayed with me, even when I moved to the city. As a teenager, I moved to New York City, where my food education took root. I ate my first avocado around a family dinner in Tribeca, and I'll never forget that intense fatty smoothness from the first bite. I ended up scraping around the bottom of the salad bowl digging for more. From New York, I moved to Seattle and my food education grew. I worked for a celebrated chef and was surrounded by food all day, every day.

I read foodie magazines, eavesdropped on kitchen conversations, and ate as much as I could. This constant exposure to food and restaurants got my little wheels turning. I was one of those really lame twenty-somethings who actually liked cooking at home. I spent nights poring over cookbooks and reading recipes as if they were gospel. I couldn't afford to eat out every night, so I tried to mock fancy restaurant dishes in my own kitchen. Or at least mock the flavors. I never was one for hours and hours of long prep and arduous recipes. I get bored too quickly. Instead, I took shortcuts, tweaked recipes using what I had in my pantry, and set off on my own private exploration of how to make food taste good.

My pantry is an ever-present character in my life. Sometimes it pulses and bulges with too many ingredients, bought with good intentions but never used. Sometimes I open it up, look at all my well-stocked shelves full of grain, fruits, nuts, and preserves, and think, "I have nothing to make." Pantries are fickle—sometimes offering a wealth of options and sometimes feeling completely bare, even when packed to the gills. Stocking a pantry takes organization. It's easy to fill it with ingredients that seem fun at the grocery store but sit untouched for months once you get them home. In my own pantry, I've been staring at the same bag of amaranth flour for far too long. It drives me crazy to waste the space and have this bag of grain taunting me every time I see it. So now I have to figure out what to make with it.

Urban Pantry aims to demystify that age-old question "What's for dinner?" It provides a creative and wholesome foundation to start thinking about food in a fresh, different, delicious way. Recipes maximize ingredients the average home cook tends to have around. If you make roast chicken one night for dinner, for example, plan on using the leftovers the next day in a panzanella salad. Making the most out of your time spent in the kitchen is a smart way to start thinking about food. And varying the ingredients considerably keeps food interesting. I'm not a culinary genius—I'm just organized. This book provides an approachable way to add more nutritious food to your meals. It all starts with your pantry and stocking it well. It *will* all taste good, which, let's be honest, is key. Living an organic, healthy, seasonal, sustainable, insert-other-eco-buzz-word-here lifestyle does not mean you have to eat boring food better served to horses. I'm a city girl through and through. I may have dirt under my nails and a farmer's tan, but I also like to drink fancy cocktails with basil-scented syrup and have champagne on a Tuesday night. Why not? Life is short. Too short for running out to the grocery at 8:00 PM because you ran out of flour and your friend can't make her fancy gravy that tastes so good over her perfectly roasted chicken. Right, Marcus?

chapter 1

stocking the pantry

I LOVE MY PANTRY. It's one of the most revered spots in my small city apartment. Only three shelves tall and three jars deep, my pantry is organized by type of food and filled with clear glass vessels in various shapes and sizes. I keep families of staples together. Grains are stacked upon other grains, and nuts and dried fruits are lined up together. The entire top shelf is piled high with preserves that I put up in season, organized left to right—a real-life calendar that mirrors the date that I pre-served. In this fashion I'm able to take a quick glance up and inventory which preserves I should be eating and which I should be hoarding. Winter citrus is consumed in summer and fall. Summer fruits are saved for holiday and winter pies. The few packaged foods I rely on adorn the middle pantry shelf and include some canned goods like tomato sauce and coconut milk, along with specialty dried noodles from Croatia, Japan, and Vietnam.

Because I live in a little place and have a tiny kitchen (only two people in at a time!), I've learned to be organized and diligent about keeping order in the pantry. It spills out well beyond the confines of those three shelves, however. My freezer is packed with dough, various stocks, and an ice cream basin. The refrigerator keeps eggs, dairy, and produce fresh. Cellared vegetables are wedged between pots and pans in cool, dark cupboards. "Pantry" simply means "a room or closet used for storage from which food is brought to the table." It does not make a distinction between dry and fresh goods. But there is a difference between *building* a pantry and *stocking* the pantry. *Building* the pantry is a chore, done over time. You build a pantry by trying new oils, experimenting with different flours, or discover-ing new spices. *Stocking* the pantry focuses on adding key ingredients and provisions so that you can actually cook a meal. A well-stocked pantry allows you to eat on demand.

Although I live smack in the middle of a city , I feel a sense of security in my well-stocked pantry. If I were to be snowed in for weeks on end, I would not go hungry. In fact, I'd be eating pretty well (and so would my neighbors). I can pull together a meal for two or three or four at a moment's notice, based solely on the goods I keep on hand. City living certainly allows me to conveniently procure food, but

I appreciate that I have the ability to hunker down and cook for myself and others in the two-foot-square space in front of my stove.

There are some practical measures I consider when stocking my pantry, outside of the desire to eat well. Call it smart economy or call it frugality, but buying whole food items in bulk is the ultimate in affordability. Whole grains, flours, sugars, spices, dried fruits, and nuts are typically available in the bulk bins of grocery stores. Not only is the cost per pound less expensive than a packaged good, but purchasing these items in small amounts also ensures freshness and hinders foods going rancid. Having to shop at the grocery every night with the looming question of what to cook for dinner is a surefire way to overpurchase and lose focus. Having said that, however, I do not prefer to sit down and plan ahead for my meals each week, either. Honestly, sometimes I don't want to think about it at all. I just want to get home and eat. Maintaining a stocked pantry ensures that there will always be something tasty just a hot pot or skillet away.

Pantry cooking demands improvisation. They say that necessity is the mother of invention, and this is certainly true when you're hungry and staring at three shelves of foodstuffs. Those canned goods come in handy on such occasions, and I often let the food that I've preserved dictate my meals. Following is a list of the pantry goods that I always keep handy. These items go above and beyond the basic pantry staples of all-purpose flour, granulated sugar, salt, and so on. Instead, they either add big flavor, increase the health value of traditional pantry goods, or act as a base from which to start off a recipe.

FLOURS

I try to keep a well-rounded inventory of flours in my pantry for both the flavor differences and the inspiration. If I have them around, staring me in the face, I will use them in some way. I rely on all-purpose flour less and less in my cooking, opting for whole wheat flour more often. The flavor is markedly different, but over time I've adapted and have grown to love other, more nutritious flours.

EMMER FLOUR. Also known as farro, emmer is a heritage whole grain (an open-pollinated seed, non-GMO variety). The germ is left behind in the milling process, so it is a true whole grain flour. Emmer is a great second option to whole wheat pastry flour for adding a whole grain to such baked goods as quick breads, chocolate desserts, or cookies. Emmer is soft enough for baking and has a nearly sweet flavor, so it won't give off a slight sourness in the final product as a wheat flour tends to do.

FLAX MEAL. An indisputable source of soluble and insoluble fiber, flax contains omega-3 fatty acids. I use flax as an oil replacement in some baked goods (read the packaging for proportions and directions) and put a few spoonfuls in my morning yogurt or *batido* (icy milk drink). Store flax meal in an airtight container in the fridge.

SEMOLINA FLOUR. This is a coarse grind of durum wheat flour. I keep a small bag in my freezer, as I don't use it often, but it's a key ingredient in home pasta making. Semolina flour can also be used for dusting the bottoms of pizza crusts (so they don't stick) or for thickening soups.

WHOLE WHEAT PASTRY FLOUR. This has a softer body (as it is milled finer) than pure whole wheat flour and can therefore be added to baked goods without having them get too dense or heavy. I substitute half the all-purpose flour in my recipes with whole wheat pastry flour to add a little whole grain goodness.

SUGARS

Outside of granulated sugar lies a rainbow of options for sweetening up meals. More often than not, it is granulated sugar that is used in these recipes—any other sugars are called out specifically in the recipe lists.

CASTER SUGAR. This finely ground cane sugar is used in recipes in which it is crucial to have your sugar melt, as with meringue (for example, see Pavlova in chapter 5, "Cooking with Eggs") or caramel. You can purchase caster sugar in specialty food shops, but I never spend money on purchasing it ready made. Instead, grind regular cane sugar in the blender to a fine consistency, near powder. Store any extra in your cupboards, in an airtight resealable container.

FAIR-TRADE ORGANIC CANE SUGAR. I'm calling this sugar out because it is leaps and bounds better than the overprocessed, bleached white sugar that many of us grew up on. God bless organics and fair trade, which allow small farmers to pay for organic certification. Now you can buy "regular" sugar that is good, instead of brands traditionally grown with pesticides. Try to purchase in bulk to save a pretty penny or two. Organic cane sugar is indispensable for baking.

HONEY. Purchasing honey from a local beekeeper is your best bet for pantry stocking. Local honey is made from local pollen. Eating this may help your body adjust to the seasons come springtime when the air is full of pollen—it's a natural allergy deterrent! Honey adds a subtle sweetness to recipes. I use it often in vinaigrettes and over my morning cereal or yogurt bowl.

TURBINADO OR DEMERARA SUGAR. Large sugar crystals make this sugar the perfect crisp and sweet garnish for finishing off cookies, tarts, and other desserts (see Almond–Butter Tart in chapter 6, "Nuts"). They are sometimes called sanding sugars, although traditional sanding sugars tend to be smaller crystals. You will not use demerara often, but when you do, nothing compares.

Storage in the Pantry

Over time, as you continue adding to your pantry, storage becomes an issue. Cupboards are prime real estate and must house infinite combinations of packaging, jars, and container sizes. To streamline the pantry so you can easily see what you have on hand, I recommend using glass jars of various sizes. I use canning jars for practically everything—preserves, scented sugars, and storage of foodstuffs in my fridge—and I never run short. I prefer to hold things in glass jars as opposed to plastic containers, as the plastic picks up aromas and oils over time. Besides, glass jars just look cooler! If you keep small jars on hand, you're apt to save little leftovers instead of throwing them out. I make it a habit to never throw any edible food away; instead, I jar it and resolve to use the leftovers in some creative way. You can also reuse glass jars—from housing spices to mayo to various small bites—but you can't reuse a piece of plastic wrap.

Another great storage tip is to reuse resealable plastic bags. They wash and dry easily (just turn them inside out and place on a drying rack) and do the best job of keeping moisture in food. This is important when you are storing items like cured meat or cheese. Produce bags from the grocery store work wonders as well for keeping dried or frozen goods fresh; they are airtight and conform to the shape of whatever is being stored. However, plastic bags are not recommended for storing fresh vegetables and fruit. Most produce does better with a little moisture and some air circulation. The crispers in refrigerators tend to do a good job of keeping moisture in, but to extend the life of produce, remove it from the produce bags. Fresh greens can be wrapped in single layers of slightly dampened linen towels. Apples can be kept in paper bags (although they do very well individually wrapped in tissue paper and stored in the garage), and herbs can be kept as you would fresh flowers—in small jars with an inch or so of water that is refreshed every other day. Most other vegetables should either be stored in the crisper on their own or wrapped loosely with a dish towel.

CHOCOLATE

There are two essential chocolate items you need in your pantry to whip up a quick dessert or embellish with some cocoa goodness—bittersweet chocolate and cocoa powder. With these two ingredients, you can make anything.

CHOCOLATE. Chocolate, particularly the bittersweet variety, should be a staple in any pantry. Keep a bar in cool, dark place, and you'll always be ready to make a sultry dessert. Bars are better than chips as they tend to keep longer—and you'll be less prone to snack!

COCOA POWDER. A must-have in your pantry if you like to bake, cocoa powder lends a rich chocolate flavor to recipes and can be used with both sweet and savory dishes. Cocoa can be dusted on desserts (like Pavlova in chapter 5, "Cooking with Eggs" and Chocolate Buttermilk Cake in chapter 2, "Milk & Yogurt") for a pretty presentation and subtle chocolate taste. I keep a small airtight jar handy, and it lasts a long time.

OILS & FATS

My pantry is overflowing with a variety of oils—vegetable, olive, nuts, and so on. Oils impart unique flavor to a dish, but should also be selected because of their smoke points. Some oils can be cooked at a higher heat than others and are therefore used in certain recipes. Hands down, I could not live without olive oil. If you must choose one, stick with olive oil and you can't go wrong.

COCONUT OIL. This is a big splurge for the pantry (so make sure to lick the spoon after you scoop some), but worth every cent. Coconut oil has a high smoke point, meaning it takes a *lot* of heat to burn. It's a stable oil that lends a very subtle coconut flavor to dishes. I use it when cooking something vegetarian, as it has a nice full-fat feel that is very satisfying (see Hippie Hotcakes and Barley & Sweet Potato Salad, both in chapter 3, "Whole Grains").

EXTRA VIRGIN OLIVE OIL. I use olive oil every day in my kitchen. In fact, I don't use many other oils, as olive oil works well for most everything. I recommend purchasing a "nice" olive oil—one you'll use raw, in vinaigrettes or drizzled on soup. If you can taste before you buy, even better. Choose something fruity and nutty and fresh-tasting. It's also a good idea to stock an "everyday" olive oil—one you'll use to coat pans and sauté vegetables. With this type of use, the olive oil flavor often won't shine through, so you can get away with something a bit cheaper. For my everyday olive oil, I purchase organic extra virgin from California in bulk from my co-op; I buy a big tin of Italian olive oil for the good stuff.

SCHMALTZ AND BACON FAT. Fat rendered from poultry is known as schmaltz. It's a great way to flavor your meals and extend your dollars. Pour fat from the pan after roasting a chicken, and store it in a jar in the fridge. Save any leftover bacon fat, making sure to save only the clear fat—those small brown bits at the bottom of a jar are quite unsightly. Bacon fat can be used in sautéing or cooking eggs, lending the smoky flavor of bacon without all the calories.

WINE, VINEGAR & BOOZE

Acid is a very important element to any dish—one that seldom gets recognized as being important to a novice cook. Vinegar, therefore, is an absolute pantry staple. Ditto for wines and liqueurs, which are consummate recipe wonders. They add something extra to recipes, and I'm always sure to have a few small bottles around. Keep all of these in a cool, dark cupboard away from a heat source like your stove, to increase shelf life and maintain flavors.

APPLE CIDER VINEGAR. This vinegar is great for those instances when I need a little acid in a gravy or sauce, but I don't have a lemon around. When I'm preserving and pickling, I often turn to apple cider vinegar (see Indian Pickled Carrots in chapter 1, "Stocking the Pantry," and Ajvar and Apricot Mustard in chapter 8, "Small-Batch Preserving"). I buy a huge gallon container at the start of summer and use it up over the course of the season.

COGNAC AND KIRSCH. Pick up small travel-sized bottles of these from the liquor store and keep them tucked into the corner of your cupboard. These sweet liqueurs are called for in baking or cooking, and I'm always grateful that I have them on hand. A little tablespoon really does make a difference in a recipe (see Simple Pecan Crumble & Baked Apples in chapter 6, "Nuts").

RED WINE VINEGAR. A go-to for vinaigrettes, red wine vinegar has a sharp bite that wakes up not-very-flavorful ingredients like grains or bean salads (see Bulgur & Citrus Salad in chapter 3, "Whole Grains," and Lentils with Mint & Beets in chapter 4, "Beans & Peas").

RICE WINE VINEGAR. This is my favorite vinegar, as it packs an acidic bite while also having a soft sweetness. I use rice wine vinegar in quick pickles (see Cucumber Quick Pickles in chapter 1, "Stocking the Pantry") and Asian dressings (especially the thick peanut sauce in Peanut Soba Noodles in chapter 4, "Beans & Peas") and even in vinaigrettes for simple green salads.

SHERRY. Sherry is a fortified wine (brandy is added after fermentation) and tastes sweet and boozy. I use it to deglaze my pans when I'm cooking something savory like pan gravy (it's my secret ingredient) or sautéing vegetables; the sherry serves as a bit of acid when I don't have fresh lemon juice available. Nice for sipping, too. (See Pearled Barley Risotto with Sherried Mushrooms & Leeks in chapter 3, "Whole Grains.")

VERMOUTH. Use dry white vermouth for deglazing pans and for lending richness to soups, stocks, and sauces (see Vegetable Scrap Stock and Rich Tomato Gravy in chapter 2, "Kitchen Economy").

SHAOXING WINE. I use this Chinese cooking wine for marinating meats and making soups. Use two parts stock to one part Shaoxing for a fragrant and soothing broth. Add some noodles and chopped green onions, and you have a nutritious meal.

DRIED FRUITS

Dried figs, dates, apricots, and raisins are excellent pantry staples. In combination, dried fruits work together in baked goods or as sides to main courses. On their own, they are sweet additions to savory salads (Apricot–Chickpea Salad in chapter 4, "Beans & Peas") and morning shakes (Batidos in chapter 7, "Milk & Yogurt").

READY-TO-EAT GOODIES

Having foodstuffs in your pantry is one of the single most important things you can do to cook easily at home. It's not cooking that is hard—it is the running around gathering ingredients that is exhausting. Be sure to keep a few basics around so you're able to cook impromptu meals.

FROZEN PUFF PASTRY SHEETS. I use these when I need to pull together a dessert or an appetizer quickly, like the caramelized Onion–Thyme Tart (in chapter 2, "Kitchen Economy"). Puff pastry sheets defrost quickly and taste fantastic. They are a bit of a chore to make from scratch, so I prefer to purchase this item. Wrapped airtight, puff pastry will keep in the freezer indefinitely. Sheets can be defrosted and frozen again if unused.

BACON. I keep a pound of slab bacon in my freezer and cut off little bits at a time for cooking. It's great in a pot of beans or lentils (for example, see Bones & Beans in chapter 2, "Kitchen Economy").

PROSCIUTTO. Like bacon but even easier to use (it requires no cooking time), prosciutto is wonderful warmed up in a pan with melted butter for a quick pasta sauce. Or for a fast meal, layer some on toast with a fried egg. Keep prosciutto wrapped tightly in plastic so it does not dry out.

SMOKED FISH. I turn to smoked salmon and smoked trout when I don't have the time or energy to cook a protein (see Lovage & Smoked Salmon Hard-Boiled Eggs in chapter 5, "Cooking with Eggs"). Cured and smoked, fish has a long shelf life in the fridge if stored properly. Once opened, be sure to wrap smoked fish tightly with plastic wrap and refrigerate it in an airtight container or plastic bag.

LOOSE TEA. I'm a big fan of infusing tea into food, in preserves or dried fruit (see "Steeping Fruit" in this chapter). I also enjoy drinking a big hot cup every now and again. Keep a healthy selection at hand so you have flexibility in your cooking. Stock one handful each of green tea, black tea, and an herbal tea of your liking (chamomile or mint complement a wide variety of flavors). Steep these in reusable small canvas tie-string bags (available where you purchase loose tea).

VEGETABLE BOUILLON. Let me say this right off the bat: I do not like bouillon cubes. They are too salty and don't taste like proper stock at all. Generally I try to have homemade stock on hand at all times (Resourceful Chicken Stock and Vegetable Scrap Stock in chapter 2, "Kitchen Economy"). However, in a pinch, they are great to have around. Bouillon cubes have saved me on more than one occasion. Purchase a brand with the fewest number of ingredients listed on the package, and steer clear of any bouillon with weird chemical names in the ingredients list. I opt for bouillon cubes over stock in cans or cartons, as they take up less space in the pantry.

COCONUT MILK. I love the flavor of coconut milk and I love Asian food, so I always keep a can around. Use coconut milk in soups (Carrot–Coconut Milk Soup in chapter 6, "Nuts") in place of broth.

COCONUT FLAKES. Whether full flakes or shredded coconut, be sure to purchase the unsweetened version of this item. Coconut flakes are a super flavor booster in morning shakes, over a bowl of yogurt (with some dried fruit), or tossed into curry. Store coconut flakes in an airtight container in the pantry.

TOMATOES. Tomatoes are the one fruit that I do not (often) preserve in summer. Canned tomatoes are readily available and affordable, so I purchase a few cans at a time and keep them handy for when I don't have fresh produce available. Buy organic canned tomatoes and opt for tomatoes that have no added flavor or salt. (You can always add flavor and salt on your own.) If you have time on your hands and can preserve tomatoes, I highly endorse the endeavor. Be sure to keep a tube of tomato paste in your fridge as well. The tube version minimizes waste from opened cans and keeps for a long while after opening.

DIJON MUSTARD. This strong, smooth mustard is a must for vinaigrettes with a bite and for dressing legume salads (Apricot–Chickpea Salad in chapter 4, "Beans & Peas").

FRESH PANTRY

Keep basic fresh foodstuffs in your pantry and at your fingertips year-round. They are the foundational ingredients for a large library of recipes and often store well in the pantry.

ONION. A base in so many dishes, you should always have plenty around. Store them in a cool, dark cupboard. If an onion sprouts, use the green as you would a scallion, although the inner core of the sprout is sometimes bitter and may need to be composted. If part of an onion goes rotten, trim off the spoil and use the remainder.

CARROTS AND CELERY. Many stocks, soups, and sauces start with carrot, celery, and onions, known as the basic *mirepoix* (pronounced "meer-pwa"). If you have these three ingredients, you can pull from your pantry legumes to make a meal or turn plain old water into soup. Carrots keep a long time if stored in either a cool, dark cupboard or the vegetable crisper of your fridge, but if they go soft, use them in stocks or soups. Celery should be stored in the vegetable crisper and keeps well. If celery turns brown and wilts, use a vegetable peeler to remove any brown spots, shed slimy leaves, and rinse under cool water before using.

GARLIC. With a little garlic and some olive oil, you can coax any vegetable into a tasty sauté. Store garlic in a cool, dark cupboard. As with an onion, if garlic sprouts, taste a sprout to see if you like the flavor. If not, cut it from the clove and use the garlic as you normally would.

POTATOES. Almost all varieties of potatoes store well in a cellared environment. If you have a cool garage, keep them there, in a paper or burlap bag. If not, choose a dark, dry, and cool cupboard in the house for your potatoes. If they sprout but remain firm, cut away the sprouts and prepare as usual. If they have sprouted and are soft and wrinkled, potatoes are best sent to the compost bin.

LEMONS. Lemons are used in nearly all preserving recipes and as a balancing acid for vinaigrettes, sautés, and salads. Choose organic lemons when you can, so the peel is free of pesticide residue.

GINGER. Use ginger in vinaigrettes, Asian- and Indian-inspired recipes, and as a base for Fizzy Ginger Soda (see chapter 8, "Small-Batch Preserving"). Ginger makes a potent infusion for custards and teas as well. The root keeps for weeks if stored in a cool, dark cupboard.

FRESH HERBS. Italian flat-leaf parsley is by far the most widely available fresh herb and also the one I use most often. When all else fails, chopped fresh parsley garnish over a finished dish provides a fresh, clean bite. Store the fresh-cut herb in a glass, filled with an inch of water. Replenish the water every other day or so, just as you would for a floral bouquet. In this fashion you can keep parsley fresh for more than a week. See chapter 9, "The Pantry Garden," for extensive information on other fresh herb suggestions. Note that dried herbs lose their flavor quickly and therefore should only be purchased when specifically called for in a recipe.

stocking the pantry
{ RECIPES }

There are certain recipes that I use time and time again—so much so that I nearly have them memorized. I keep them in a handwritten notebook on top of my refrigerator, so I have them within quick reach while cooking. Flipping through the notebook's worn and oil-stained pages is a cherished exercise. It's always eye-opening to review the dishes I've made and loved in the past. Not just anything makes it into the notebook, however; recipes have to earn their place. I've come to think of this collection as my kitchen essentials—classic preparations that emerge from a well-stocked pantry. With some advance preparation and the proper storing techniques, these delicious essentials guarantee a homemade meal that is ready in a snap. They build on basic items already in your pantry. As with any home project, you need to invest some time to make these enhanced ingredients. But once created and stocked, they will add that something special to your meals. These handmade items are meant to marry ingredients you already have on hand with food that you're cooking in the hopes of nailing the perfect bite. Mastering the concept behind quick pickles, infusions, and fruit syrups, for example, builds up a repertoire of key techniques and flavor combinations that you can work from and make your own variations with over time.

Whole Grain Bread

[MAKES 1 LOAF]

This bread is not for the faint of heart. This is the black coffee of bread—dense and heavy. If you dropped this loaf on your foot, you'd likely do some damage. Purchase only as much flour as you need for this recipe, so you don't have extra to store. You can easily double this recipe and freeze a second loaf. Best eaten as toast, or as a sturdy bottom to an open-faced sandwich, this bread is an excellent staple to have in your pantry. You may substitute emmer flour for barley flour.

1 teaspoon active dry yeast
1½ cups warm water
2 tablespoons honey
1½ teaspoons salt
1½ cups barley flour
2 to 4 cups whole wheat flour, divided
1 tablespoon unsalted butter, melted

In a small bowl, dissolve the active dry yeast in the warm water and set aside for 10 to 15 minutes, or until foamy. Stir in the honey and salt until incorporated.

Using a standing mixer fitted with a dough hook, combine the barley flour, 2 cups of the whole wheat flour, yeast mixture, and the butter for 5 to 6 minutes on medium slow, or until all the flour is incorporated.

Remove the dough from the mixer and put it on a well-floured (with whole wheat flour) work surface. Knead for 5 to 8 minutes, until the dough is elastic and smooth. Add as much whole wheat flour as necessary, but don't incorporate more than another 2 cups here. The dough will be tacky to the touch. Place the dough in a large bowl, cover with plastic wrap or a damp dish towel, and set in a warm spot until it doubles in size, usually about 2 to 4 hours.

Punch down the dough and place it in a loaf pan (approximately 9 inches by 5 inches). Cover with plastic wrap or a damp dish towel and let the dough rise a second time, until it hits the top of the pan, usually another 1 to 2 hours. (If you do not have a loaf pan, free-form a batard-shaped loaf, put it on a sheet pan, and cover as directed.)

Preheat the oven to 350 degrees F. Place the loaf pan on the center rack and bake for about 40 to 50 minutes, or until the bread browns lightly. The loaf should fall easily from the pan when tapped and sound hollow when you knock on the bottom. Cool slightly before serving.

PANTRY NOTE: Store baked whole grain bread in a plastic bag in your fridge, where it will keep for about two weeks. If the bread turns stale, slice it thin and bake for 7 to 10 minutes at 350 degrees for a crispy homemade crostini. You can also store baked bread in a plastic bag in the freezer, where it will keep for two to three months.

Hand-Rolled Pasta

[MAKES 1½ POUNDS PASTA, OR 4 TO 6 SERVINGS]

Some people shy away from making homemade pasta, as it seems like an impossible chore. Most urban kitchens do not have room for a pasta machine, but if grannies in Italy can roll out their pasta by hand, I figure I can too. Rolling out the dough is a bit of a workout but shouldn't take more than 10 minutes, at most. This pasta dough uses a bare minimum of ingredients, doesn't need much drying time, and cooks up easily. From start to finish, you'll need 2 hours total.

> 2 cups all-purpose flour
> 1 cup semolina flour
> 5 eggs

Mix all of the ingredients in a standing mixer fitted with a dough hook on low speed for about 5 minutes, or until the dough comes together and is fairly smooth. Turn it out onto a lightly floured countertop and knead by hand about 3 to 4 minutes, until the dough is elastic and shiny. Wrap it tightly in plastic wrap and refrigerate for at least 30 minutes and up to 1 hour.

Remove the dough from the fridge and divide it into three equal pieces. Using one piece at a time (and keeping the others well wrapped in plastic wrap), shape the dough into a flattened rectangular disc . Lightly flour your workspace and roll out the dough, keeping its rectangular shape as much as possible (don't worry too much if the dough takes on a different shape). Roll it out until quite thin—about 20 to 22 inches long and 8 to 10 inches wide (be sure to turn the dough over occasionally and roll the other side). Dust your workspace as needed so the dough does not stick. It should be thin, like a stick of gum, and should take about 8 minutes to roll out. Using a pastry brush, remove any excess flour.

To cut your noodles, fold the dough, lengthwise, into a 5-inch-wide rectangular roll. Using a sharp knife, cut the noodles thin (for fettuccine) or thick (for tagliatelle). Unfold the roll and hang the noodles to dry, for at least 10 minutes and up to 30 minutes. I hang my pasta on a string tied between the backs of two chairs, but any thin stringlike option will work—a dowel rod, a hanger, a lampshade, and so on.

Just before serving, bring a pot of heavily salted water to boil. Add a handful of pasta and cook 8 to 10 minutes, until al dente but not too toothsome. Drain and serve immediately, or use any leftover pasta in Herbal Minestrone (see recipe in chapter 4, "Beans & Peas").

PANTRY NOTE: Fully dried hand-rolled pasta may be stored in an airtight container for up to two months. You can also freeze pasta by twirling freshly cut noodles into small rounds, placing them in a plastic bag, and sprinkling with semolina flour (to prevent sticking). Hand-rolled pasta will keep in the freezer indefinitely but is best used within four months.

Whole Wheat Tart & Pie Dough

[MAKES TWO 9-INCH SHELLS]

I always try to incorporate some measure of whole grain into my cooking. With flour, however, the coarse texture of a whole grain is often too heavy for most pastries. I found a solution in whole wheat pastry flour—a lighter option. It allows for the use of a whole grain flour but is milled softer and works well to turn out a delicate pastry. For this recipe I combine half all-purpose flour with half whole wheat pastry flour for a healthier version of a traditional pantry staple. The trick to tart dough is not to overprocess it in the mixer. You want to see big hunks of butter in the dough, which leads to a crispy, flaky tart or pie crust. This recipe is super for both sweet tarts (Almond–Butter Tart in chapter 6, "Nuts") and savory tarts. Make a double batch of dough and store some in your freezer, rolled out to fit in your favorite pie dish or to make rustic individual hand-formed tarts.

> 1 cup all-purpose flour
> 1 cup whole wheat pastry flour
> 1 teaspoon salt
> 1 teaspoon sugar
> 2 sticks (½ pound) chilled unsalted butter, cut into small cubes
> 8 tablespoons ice water

Put all of the dry ingredients into a food processor, and pulse once or twice to combine. Add the butter and pulse just until the dough forms large crumbles—be careful not to overmix. (Typically, I pulse between 30 and 38 times.)

Pour in the ice water and pulse until just combined and the dough starts to come together in two or three large portions. This takes about 8 to 10 seconds, so be mindful not to overprocess.

Turn the dough out onto a countertop and divide in half, pressing each half into two flat round discs, each about 6 inches in diameter. Be careful not to work the dough. Wrap each piece tightly in plastic wrap and refrigerate for at least 2 hours before rolling out.

When ready to use, remove dough from the fridge. Lightly flour a work surface. Using a rolling pin, roll out the dough into about a 10-inch round (be sure to rotate the dough and flip over, rolling both sides). Keep your work surface lightly floured so the dough does not stick.

Fold the round in half and place over a 9 x 1-inch tart pan with a removable bottom (the crease of the dough should run down the middle of the pan). Unfurl the dough so it hangs over the edge of the tart pan. Press it gently into the corners of the tart pan, being careful not to stretch it too thin. Turn any overhanging crust under and press it into the walls of the tart pan. Run your rolling pin over the top of the pan, pressing down to trim any extra dough. Pierce the bottom of the tart shell with a fork in several places. Put the pan and tart shell in the freezer for 30 minutes before baking.

Preheat the oven to 350 degrees F. Remove the pan and tart shell from the freezer and line the inside with parchment paper. Put pie weights or beans on the parchment paper, pressing into the corners. Bake on the center rack for 20 minutes. Remove the pie weights and parchment and bake for another 10 to 15 minutes, until golden brown. Remove the tart shell from the oven and cool until ready to use.

PANTRY NOTE: This dough holds for three days in the fridge. Prebaked shells will hold for three days at room temperature, loosely wrapped in parchment paper. Alternatively, you can roll out the dough into one big disc, wrap tightly in plastic wrap, fold it into quarters, and store in the freezer for up to a month. When ready to use, thaw in the fridge overnight and bake as instructed.

Homemade Bread Crumbs

[MAKES ABOUT 2 CUPS]

This recipe works best when the loaf of bread is one or two days old, but I've also used fresh bread with good results. Rustic bakery loaves are my favorite, but most bread will do just fine. The point is to use up the bits of baguette and bread that you inevitably have left over after a meal. I, for one, seldom remember to wrap it up and store it properly, so I'm often whipping up a batch of these fragrant bread crumbs. Play with the proportions by increasing or decreasing quantities, depending on how much bread you have or your flavor preference.

½ loaf leftover bread, cut into 1-inch cubes
3 teaspoons kosher salt
1 teaspoon freshly ground black pepper
6 sprigs fresh thyme, leaves picked and chopped
1 branch fresh rosemary, leaves picked and chopped
3 sprigs fresh sage, leaves picked and chopped
¼ cup olive oil

Preheat the oven to 375 degrees F. Put the bread cubes on a sheet pan. Sprinkle the salt, black pepper, thyme, rosemary, and sage and drizzle with the olive oil. Using your hands, toss the mixture until the bread is coated well. The croutons should feel moist but not saturated with oil.

Bake until the croutons are golden brown, tossing as needed, for about 20 minutes. Remove from the oven and cool. When the croutons are cool, put them and the herby crumbs from the sheet pan into the basin of a food processor. Pulse until the crumbs resemble a coarse meal or finer if preferred. Use these as a stuffing (see Stuffing: Savory Fillings in this chapter) or to fry up a chicken cutlet.

PANTRY NOTE: These bread crumbs will keep for four to six weeks before getting a wee bit stale. Store them in a glass jar in your cupboard. Be sure the bread crumbs are cool and dry; moisture from steam will turn them stale if you store them too quickly. You can also make unseasoned bread crumbs quickly by pulsing crusty bread in a food processor—just remember to season with salt, pepper, and dried herbs if desired before using.

Stuffing:
Savory Fillings

"Stuffing" seems like a very old-fashioned word. It immediately calls to mind holiday feasts, moms cooking roasts, and big family dinners around a large table. But stuffing isn't just about croutons and turkey. The best stuffing, in fact, takes the simplest ingredients and turns them into something unexpected and complex. A mix of finely chopped fresh herbs, a paste of ground nuts, or a handful of crispy bread crumbs are simple starting points for putting together a stuffing. Embellish from there by adding a bit of the outer peel from a lemon or lime for fish, or chopped dried fruits when roasting meats. Olive oil can be added to make more of a paste-like consistency.

Pounded-out meats are an easy vehicle for stuffing. The flat surface provides real estate to place the stuffing on and allows you to roll and tie the ends together, so that the stuffing stays intact and picks up the meat's full flavor—much like it does when you stuff a bird. Try a fruit infusion (see Steeping Fruit in this chapter) and add a few spoonfuls of fresh bread crumbs and garlic for a stuffing fit for pork. Purchase a thick-cut chop, slice it in the midsection (without cutting through), then stuff and tie it off. If you feel more confident in the kitchen, butterfly a pork loin and do the same. You can also pound out chicken breasts and flank steaks, then stuff and tie.

Hollowed-out fruits and vegetables are also excellent carriages. Apples can be cored and stuffed with something savory like leftover Barley & Sweet Potato Salad (in chapter 3, "Whole Grains") or something sweet like Simple Pecan Crumble & Baked Apples (in chapter 6, "Nuts"). Zucchini split lengthwise and whole bell peppers are another healthy option. You can also use steamed kale, chard, or cabbage leaves, laying them flat, then filling and folding to close. Many Middle Eastern recipes make stuffing from whole grains (such as bulgur or barley) by simply adding some onion and spices. This is an excellent way to reuse leftover grains. What's in your pantry? Try the following combinations:

FOR STUFFING APPLES

2 parts sautéed onion
2 parts bread crumbs
1 part chopped fresh thyme
1 part olive oil
Salt and pepper

or

2 parts sautéed onion
2 parts leftover cooked barley
1 part olive oil
1 part chopped fresh thyme
1 part chopped fresh sage
1 part chopped dried fruit
Salt and pepper

FOR STUFFING BEEF

2 parts chopped pine nuts
1 part diced raisins
1 part sherry vinegar
1 part olive oil
2 parts chopped fresh parsley
1 part grated lemon peel
1 part minced fresh garlic

FOR STUFFING FISH

2 parts sautéed onion
1 part chopped fresh thyme
1 part crumbled cooked bacon
1 part olive oil

or

2 parts chopped fresh parsley
2 parts chopped almonds
1 part grated lemon peel
1 part minced fresh garlic
1 part olive oil

FOR STUFFING PORK

2 parts chopped dried fruit
2 parts chopped fresh thyme
1 part olive oil

or

2 parts chopped apples
2 parts bread crumbs
2 parts olive oil
1 part chopped fresh sage

Berry Syrup

[MAKES 1 CUP]

Why stick to basic maple when you can make your own syrup at home? I learned this technique from my friend Patric, a trained pastry chef who never seems to mind dirtying all the equipment in the kitchen for one little recipe. (But it's always worth it in the end.) Any fresh or frozen berry works well here—my favorites are blueberries, raspberries, and blackberries. This recipe is perfect for Hippie Hotcakes (in chapter 3, "Whole Grains") and is also a great topping for ice cream. Ladling a berry syrup over plain-old pudding or custard is an easy way to fancy it up. Try not to scrimp on the grated lime peel—it makes all the difference!

1 cup berries, fresh or frozen
Sugar
Grated lime peel

In a small saucepan, heat berries and a few spoonfuls of sugar, along with a splash of water, over low heat until berry juices start to release. Pull the berry–sugar mixture from the heat and let cool for a moment. Divide the mixture and reserve half. Purée the other half in a blender until smooth. Pour it through a strainer to remove the skins and seeds (you can compost these).

Put the strained syrup back in the saucepan and heat over low heat. Grate in a bit of lime peel and cook until just heated through. Add the remaining whole berries and heat until about to burst, 4 to 6 minutes. Remove from heat and serve immediately.

PANTRY NOTE: Follow the same instructions with just about any berry. Try varying the citrus as well. Strawberries love orange, and raspberries love lemon. This berry syrup will keep refrigerated for two weeks, or frozen in an airtight container for four to six weeks.

Steeping Fruit

[MAKES 4 SERVINGS, AS GARNISH]

Rather than serving simple dried fruits on a cheese platter, I mix it up a bit and prepare macerated dried fruit. This infusion works well on a variety of dried fruits—raisins, apricots, and figs, for example. You can easily double this recipe and serve it over yogurt or alongside roasted or grilled meats. This fruit is also great as dessert on its own, with a little whipped cream after a big meal, when you crave just a few bites of something sweet.

1 1/2 cups water

1 Earl Grey tea bag, or a bag of loose tea

Grated peel from 1 orange

1 cinnamon stick

1/4 cup sugar

1/2 pound (about 2 cups) dried fruit, such as prunes, figs,
   apricots, or raisins

Few splashes of brandy

In a small saucepan over medium-high, heat the water, tea bag, orange peel, cinnamon stick, and sugar, until nearly boiling. Remove the mixture from the heat and stir in the dried fruit and brandy. Let it steep for at least 30 minutes, or until all the liquid is absorbed. Serve the infusion at room temperature.

PANTRY NOTE: You can easily add to this infusion. Try some cloves, different teas, or liqueurs such as cognac or sambuca. Store leftover fruit infusions in an airtight container in the fridge for up to three weeks.

Quick Pickles

Quick pickles are called "quick pickles" because they offer a way to pickle something, you know, quickly. I stole this idea from many a chef (who use quick pickles as garnish), and I keep it interesting by changing my pickling liquid. A brine is technically a salt-based soaking liquid, but with quick pickles I like to add sugar and go for something sweeter, making these more of a cure. Either way, if you can't get enough of the salty goodness a proper pickle provides, go to town and add more salt. Quick pickles are an excellent way to add color to a dish. The acid in the vinegar brightens the color of the produce you're using, and suddenly everything goes from colorful to *colorful*. In addition to being a bright little pop on your plate, these pickles bring big flavor, particularly the pickled peppers. I love the spice in red serrano peppers and green jalapeños, but I can seldom tolerate the heat they give off. A few minutes in vinegar, however, and they are a bit softer on your taste buds and more mellow with their heat.

There are two techniques to a quick pickle: In the first, you heat pickling liquid and pour it over the prepared vegetable or fruit; in the second, you simply throw everything into a bowl and let it cure in vinegar by giving it a stir once in a while. I opt for heating up the pickling liquid when I am curing a hard vegetable like carrots or celery, but I'll use the cool-pickle cure on softer produce such as cucumbers or apples. Traditional pickles that I preserve are made with apple cider vinegar. In the case of quick pickles, however, I typically default to rice wine vinegar—an ingredient commonly found in Asian cooking (see Cucumber Quick Pickles in this chapter). It has some punch but lacks the bite I've come to expect from traditional white vinegar. White vinegar is another great option, though. It is intense but readily available, and because it does not spend too much time on the vegetables, it works. (White vinegar also has high acidity and is therefore safe to use in canning.) One vinegar to steer clear of in quick pickling is balsamic vinegar. Balsamic is not actually a wine vinegar; rather, it is made from grape pressings and then aged. It lacks the acid of the other vinegars, so save this one for your salads.

Because quick pickles are made with an acid, you have to be a tad bit selective about what to serve them with; pairings are suggested here. I love myself some quick pickles. They are powerful little things—they come together in minutes, taste fantastic, and look beautiful. I could go on for days. Please try these. You will fall in love.

Carrot Quick Pickles

[MAKES 4 TO 6 SIDE-DISH SERVINGS]

For firmer produce such as carrots, celery, or fennel bulbs, quick pickles work best if the pickling liquid is heated and thereby actually cooks the veggies a bit. In this version I include my favorite ingredients for quick pickling, borrowed from Seattle chef Tom Douglas. As with most quick pickles, this recipe can be edited based on ingredients you have available. Omit or swap out spices and vegetables. These pickled carrots are a perfect side dish in summer, but they also go well with any braised meat or on a sandwich in place of raw onions.

> 4 carrots, peeled and thinly sliced
> 1½ cups apple cider vinegar
> 2 tablespoons sugar
> One 3-inch piece of ginger, peeled and cut into coins
> 2 whole star anise (optional)
> 1 cinnamon stick
> 1 teaspoon whole black peppercorns
> 1 teaspoon coriander seeds
> Pinch salt

Place the carrots in a nonreactive mixing bowl (one that is not metal) and set aside. In a medium saucepan, heat the apple cider vinegar, sugar, ginger, star anise, cinnamon stick, black peppercorns, coriander seeds, and salt over medium heat until simmering. When the liquid is near boiling, pour it over the carrots and let the mixture sit on the counter until cool, stirring occasionally. Serve the carrots in the brine.

PANTRY NOTE: These pickled carrots can be made ahead and stored in an airtight container (ideally a glass jar) in the fridge for up to three weeks, as long as the carrots stay submerged.

Quick Pickled Chiles

[MAKES 4 SERVINGS, AS GARNISH]

These chiles add a beautiful pop of color and a nice sweet-heat to many dishes. Serve a few thin slivers over fish fillets, or pair them with grilled meat or crispy tofu. A note of warning: Be careful not to touch your eyes or skin when working with hot chiles. Better yet: Wear rubber gloves!

> 1 tablespoon sugar
> ½ cup rice wine vinegar
> 1 fresh red pepper (paprika or serrano), stemmed, seeded,
>   cut lengthwise into thin slices
> 1 thin-skinned fresh green pepper (jalapeño or Hungarian wax),
>   stemmed, seeded, cut lengthwise into thin slices

In a small bowl, mix together the sugar and rice wine vinegar until the sugar is dissolved. Add the red pepper and green pepper to the sugar–vinegar mixture and macerate for 30 minutes or longer. The longer the peppers macerate, the less spice they will retain. Serve immediately.

PANTRY NOTE: These pickled chiles can be stored in an airtight container (a glass jar is best) in the fridge for up to three weeks, so long as the peppers stay submerged.

Cucumber Quick Pickles

[MAKES 4 SIDE-DISH SERVINGS]

In this quick pickle version I've added some Asian flavors. Try these cucumbers served alongside soba noodles (see Peanut Soba Noodles in chapter 4, "Beans & Peas").

1½ cups rice wine vinegar

3 tablespoons sugar

2 cucumbers, peeled and cut into thin slices

Few shakes of sesame oil

1 tablespoon sesame seeds (raw or toasted)

In a nonreactive bowl (one that is not metal), stir together the rice wine vinegar and sugar until the sugar is dissolved. Add the cucumbers and macerate for at least 15 minutes and up to 45 minutes, stirring every 5 minutes. When you've reached a good flavor, shake in a few drops of sesame oil. Add the sesame seeds and serve the cucumbers in the pickling liquid.

PANTRY NOTE: Omit the sesame seeds and sesame oil, and this cool pickling works well for apples cut into matchsticks or red onions cut into thin rings. You may need to halve or double the recipe, depending on how many pickles you wish to make. Don't feel that you need to be precise with the measurements. If your final pickle is too sweet, splash a little more vinegar on. If it's too acidic, add a few spoonfuls of sugar until the taste is to your liking.

chapter 2

kitchen economy

I STARTED A CASUAL CANNING SOCIETY among friends last year. I invited food lovers, an eco-minded peer who wanted to eat local all year long, and a friend with a stellar kitchen to participate in a weekly "canathon." Calling ourselves the "Stockpilers," we arranged it so that each week someone picked up thirty to forty pounds of in-season produce from our local farmers markets and we all converged in the kitchen to put up preserves and can, stockpiling our pantries for the winter. One afternoon, while the group was inside loading up jars of raw-packed apricots, I found all of the pits in the compost bin. Digging through, I grabbed as many as I could, took the pile of pits outside, and with a hammer started cracking them open to reveal the inner kernel. The kernel of an apricot is often bitter and strong tasting—Italians use it to make liqueur. I use the kernels to flavor canned goods, and they can also be steeped in milk for ice cream or custard, imparting a soft almond flavor. The Stockpilers were amazed that those kernels were in the pits, and gave me kudos for being resourceful. It is the perfect example of getting every-last-bit from an ingredient.

Being resourceful in your kitchen has several benefits. Getting the most you can out of a single ingredient is incredibly economical. A bunch of fresh parsley can be used down to the last leaf. Add the leaves to Bulgur & Citrus Salad (in chapter 3, "Whole Grains") or to Gremolata (in this chapter), then save the stems for a homemade vegetable stock. This practice extends the life of a very simple ingredient. Also, making a commitment to use every last drop of something forces creativity in the kitchen. If I didn't have carrot peels and parsley stems around on a fairly regular basis, I'm sure I would not make chicken and vegetable stock as often as I do. Getting multiple uses out of one ingredient is, at its very core, using smart kitchen economy.

It is good practice to be mindful of little food scraps that are sometimes left behind and easily disposed of as waste. Food waste at home is an issue these days; it is estimated that nearly 14% of food is thrown away by the average American family. To start minimizing waste, a good rule of thumb is to ask yourself "Will I be able to use this in the future?" before throwing it out. More often than not, the answer will be yes. Bacon fat can be stored in the fridge to flavor dishes later on and should be kept instead of tossed in the bin. Jus from roasted meats can be frozen and kept for a future gravy or sauce. The fat and drippings that come off a simple roast chicken can be used in the same way. The heel from a loaf of bread can be saved for croutons or breadcrumbs. Meat bones can be re-roasted and used in soups and stocks. Even bruised fruits and vegetables can often be saved by trimming away decay.

This concept can extend well beyond your kitchen. Taking home leftovers and making something delicious, bagging up your bones and extra bread from a night out at a restaurant—these are all small measures that extend the dollar. Being economical connects you to your food on a very deep level. Kitchen economy is all about making the most food with the least amount of money. It's about being conscious of where food comes from and the care it took to grow it. It's about appreciating every last bite, minimizing waste, and considering your personal carbon footprint. Kitchen economy speaks to both a richer bank account and a richer connection with your food and the environment. It does *not* mean clipping coupons or driving around town for the best deal. Grandma said it best when she scolded: "Waste not, want not." That's the best kind of economy we can hope for.

kitchen economy

{ RECIPES }

Resourceful Chicken Stock

[MAKES APPROXIMATELY 4 TO 6 CUPS]

This recipe is called "resourceful" as it's made up of various bits and bobs you have in the kitchen and does not adhere strictly to proportions. This is an excellent way to use up pantry vegetables that are past their prime. The only thing you must have is the leftover carcass from a Perfect Roast Chicken (see recipe in this chapter). It is important to re-roast the bones to get a nice brown caramel on the bottom of your stockpot. This adds much more flavor than if you were to simply cover them with water, as you would if making stock from a fresh bird.

> Olive oil
> 1 cooked and picked chicken carcass, broken up into sections
>   small enough to fit in your stockpot
> Chicken heart and neck (reserved from whole roast chicken)
> 1 carrot, roughly chopped
> 1 yellow onion, roughly chopped
> 1 celery stalk, roughly chopped
> 1 clove garlic, smashed
> 1 fresh or dried bay leaf
> Herb stalks (any you've saved)
> Salt

Cover the bottom of a large stockpot with olive oil and heat over medium-high. When the stockpot is hot, add the chicken carcass, neck, and heart. The trick here is to not continuously stir the meat and bones, but to let them sit on the heat and caramelize, about 10 minutes, stirring only occasionally. Once the bones are brown, remove them from the stockpot and set aside.

Put the carrot, onion, celery, and garlic in the stockpot. Cook for about 5 to 10 minutes or until brown. When the veggies are caramelized, drop the chicken bones, neck, and heart back in the stockpot and cover by 2 inches with water. Add the bay leaf and herb stalks and bring all to a boil. Reduce the heat to low and simmer uncovered for an hour or up to 2 hours.

Set a fine-mesh strainer over a large mixing bowl and drain the stock from the solids. Discard the solids. (Some cities allow for animal waste to be added to the compost bin; check with your utilities company and compost the solids if allowed.) Season the stock with salt to your taste.

Cover and put the stock in the fridge until cool. Once cooled, use within three days or store in plastic containers in the freezer for up to four months.

PANTRY NOTE: Chicken stock will not necessarily go bad in your freezer, but it does have the potential to get freezer burn. To minimize risk of this, cover your stock with a layer of plastic wrap, making sure it is lying directly on the surface, before putting on the plastic container lid. I have used stock that is plenty older than four months with good results.

Vegetable Scrap Stock

[MAKES ABOUT 4 CUPS]

This vegetable stock is an excellent way to use up any random slices of veggies you have around the pantry. It also works well when you have a lot of vegetable "waste" from another recipe, like the peeled carrot skins from Indian Pickled Carrots (in chapter 8, "Small-Batch Preserving"). Use those skins in place of a whole carrot, as the peels also have a lot of flavor. This vegetable stock is not as rich as chicken stock, but it's a nice option for vegetarians. Flavor is added by deglazing the pan with some vermouth or white wine. As in the Resourceful Chicken Stock recipe (in this chapter), these proportions are flexible. The only thing you really need is some sort of allium (leek, onion, etc.), as they flavor the broth like no other vegetables can.

> Olive oil
> 1 carrot, roughly chopped
> 1 onion, roughly chopped
> 1 celery stalk, roughly chopped
> 1 clove garlic, smashed
> Splash of vermouth or dry white wine
> 1 fresh or dried bay leaf
> Herb stalks
> A few whole black peppercorns

Cover the bottom of a large stockpot with olive oil and heat over medium-high. Add the carrot, onion, celery, and garlic. The trick here is to fight the urge to stir continuously. Instead, let the vegetables sit on the heat and brown some, about 10 minutes. Splash vermouth in the pan, stirring to deglaze and scrape up all the brown bits from the bottom of the stockpot. Cover the vegetables with 2 inches of water. Add the bay leaf, herb stalks, and the peppercorns and bring the mixture to a boil.

Reduce the heat to low and cover, simmering for an hour. Set a fine-mesh strainer over a large mixing bowl and drain the stock from the solids. Compost solids. Put the stock in the fridge until cool. Once cooled, use within three days or store in plastic containers in the freezer for up to four months.

PANTRY NOTE: All frozen stocks follow the same rules. Cover the stock's surface with a layer of plastic wrap before freezing, and store for up to four months.

Bones & Beans

[MAKES 4 TO 6 SERVINGS]

My grandma, Zora, grew up during the Great Depression. She has often said, "If it weren't for beans, we would've starved to death." Her stepfather, a Slovenian, cooked beans with an onion and water and would serve them doused in oil and vinegar. When the family could afford it, they would add pork and eat a pot of pork and beans all week long. In this tradition I make it a habit to box up any leftover bones (chicken, pork, duck, etc.) when I have a meal at a restaurant. At home I flavor a big pot of beans with the bones, browning them to coax out any extra flavor. This is one-pot cooking with little fuss in the kitchen. Beans are an incredible source of protein, and they are healthy and inexpensive to boot.

Olive oil

1 onion, chopped

Leftover bone (pork chop, shank, duck—whatever is on hand)

2 or 3 slices of bacon, raw or any leftovers

Splash of vermouth or dry white wine

2 cups dried cannellini beans or other large bean,
 soaked overnight and drained

6 to 8 sage leaves, torn

2 tablespoons salt

Salt and pepper

Cover the bottom of a large stockpot with a layer of olive oil and set over medium heat. Cook and stir the onions until soft, about 5 to 7 minutes. Add the leftover bone and bacon. Cook until the bottom of the stockpot is brown, by leaving over the heat and not stirring very often. You are looking for a golden caramelization in the bottom of your pan.

Deglaze with a splash of vermouth, stirring to scrape up the brown bits. Add the cannellini beans and cover them with water by 1 1/2 inches. Add the sage leaves and bring the mixture to a boil. Stir in the salt.

Reduce the heat to simmer, and cook until the beans are soft and can be mashed with the back of a spoon, 1 to 2 hours. Most of the water will be absorbed by this time. Season with salt and pepper to your liking. Garnish with chopped fresh parsley.

PANTRY NOTE: I store my beans in the fridge in the same pot I prepared them in, or I transfer them to a small bowl covered loosely with a plate. This dish will keep in your fridge about five days. If you mash beans into a paste, you can freeze them in a small plastic container and use later for white bean dip on crostini (refresh the flavor by mashing in roasted garlic cloves and a squeeze of lemon juice). You can also refresh leftover beans by adding a handful to warmed chicken or vegetable stock with some sautéed carrots, celery, and onions.

Perfect Roast Chicken

[MAKES 4 SERVINGS (OR 2, WITH INTENTIONAL LEFTOVERS)]

Roast chicken is, hands down, one of my most favorite things to eat. Not only that, it's one of the most economical dishes to cook—it's just as delicious hot from the oven as it is served cold the next day with Hand-Whipped Aioli (in chapter 5, "Cooking with Eggs") or Walnut Sauce (in chapter 6, "Nuts"). The bones can be used for Resourceful Chicken Stock (in this chapter), the livers saved for pâté, and the jus after roasting saved and frozen for a hearty gravy (see Rich Tomato Gravy, in this chapter) and another meal.

Typically, I roast my chicken plain, using only salt and pepper for flavor, but you can't go wrong by adding root vegetables to the pan—potatoes, onions, carrots—which cook confit-style in the chicken fat. The secret to the perfect roast chicken is a very hot oven. Starting the chicken on high heat and reducing the temperature during cooking guarantees crispy skin and moist meat. Try serving it with Panzanella Salad (in this chapter) for the perfect meal.

> 1 whole chicken, 4 to 5 pounds, rinsed and patted dry
> (save the heart, neck, and liver in the freezer for chicken stock)
> Freshly ground black pepper
> Salt

Preheat the oven to 475 degrees F.

Grind fresh pepper over all sides of the chicken. Next, salt the bird on all sides and in between the joints, where the wings and legs lie. Use enough salt to cover the entire chicken. Then use a little more. When you start wondering if there is too much salt, you'll have just the right amount! If you have the time, set the chicken aside for 20 to 30 minutes before baking.

Fit the bird snugly in a deep-sided baking pan and put in the hot oven. Leave it untouched for 30 minutes. After that, without opening the oven, reduce the temperature to 375 degrees F and cook for another 45 minutes. Remove from the oven and let sit for 15 minutes before carving and serving.

Pour the cooled chicken fat and drippings into a small plastic or glass container and save in the freezer for adding to future gravies, soups, and sauces.

PANTRY NOTE: Leftover chicken should be carved and held in a plastic container (or covered tightly with plastic wrap) for up to three days in the fridge. Reserve the bones for chicken stock; any leftover chicken can be served cold throughout the week. Serve with Gremolata (in this chapter) for a refreshing garnish to wake up the flavors.

Potato Gratin with Cashew Cream

OPPOSITE

TOP LEFT Hippie Hotcakes

TOP RIGHT Mom's Soft-Boiled Eggs-n-Toast

BOTTOM Barley & Sweet Potato Salad

Making Pavlova

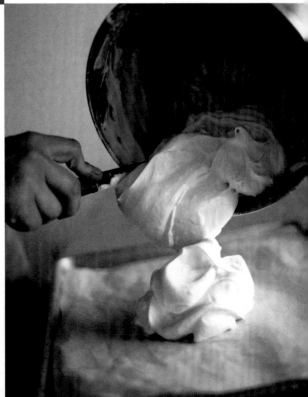

TOP LEFT Spiced Pecans
TOP RIGHT Carrot–Coconut Milk Soup
BOTTOM LEFT AND OPPOSITE Milk-Braised
Pork Shoulder with Sage

TOP LEFT Rhubarb Jam
BOTTOM RIGHT Toasted Almond Crackers
OPPOSITE, FROM LEFT TO RIGHT Boozy Blood
Orange Marmalade, Nigella Plum Jam, and
Brandy-Spiked Cherries

Preserving Hibiscus Peaches

TOP AND BOTTOM LEFT
Panzanella Salad with
Pickled Red Onions
BOTTOM RIGHT
Onion–Thyme Tart

Lovage

Tarragon

Anise hyssop

Baby lettuces

Thyme

Sage

Shiso

Beet greens

Rose geranium

Nigella

Rich Tomato Gravy

[MAKES ½ CUP GRAVY]

This gravy makes use of leftover chicken drippings, tubed tomato paste, and onions. The chicken drippings add richness to the sauce, as they would in a regular poultry gravy. Tomato paste is a fruity acid counterpoint to the fatty drippings. Together, with the onions, they make a robust "gravy" that can be used on many dishes. Pair with roasted meats, fried eggs, or as a variation of ragu for pasta.

2 tablespoons olive oil

½ onion, cut into half moons

3 cloves garlic, roughly chopped

1 teaspoon salt

1 to 2 tablespoons tomato paste

1 tablespoon white vermouth or sherry

½ cup chicken drippings

Salt and pepper

In a medium sauté pan, heat the olive oil over medium-high heat. Add the onion, garlic, and salt. Cook until the onion is soft, about 8 to 10 minutes. Stir in the tomato paste until incorporated and beginning to dry in the pan. Deglaze with the vermouth and scrape up any brown bits from the onion. Add the chicken drippings and cook down for about 5 to 10 minutes, reducing slightly until thick. Season with salt and pepper to your liking.

PANTRY NOTE: This gravy will hold in the fridge, covered in an airtight container, for up to five days. You can make this with leftover tomato sauce, instead of tomato paste, and use any leftover red wine or some balsamic vinegar in place of the vermouth or sherry.

Gremolata

[MAKES 2 TO 4 GARNISH SERVINGS]

Gremolata is a simple salad of lemon and fresh parsley. This is delicious served with slow-cooked braised meat. It's also wonderful over a whole roasted fish or chicken as the colors liven up the plate and your palate. Gremolata is a clever way to use up small portions from the pantry—a handful of salad greens, a few spoonfuls of nuts. Proportions can be toyed with in this recipe. If you'd like it really lemony, use equal parts parsley and grated lemon peel. I don't love fresh garlic, so I usually cut down on that ingredient, but if you're a fresh garlic lover, go to town!

Handful of flat-leaf Italian parsley

Lemon

1 garlic clove, minced

Chop the parsley until medium-coarse or fine (just don't leave it too rustic) and place in a small bowl. Using a rasp, grate the lemon peel into the parsley, avoiding the white pith. (If you don't own a rasp, use a vegetable peeler to remove lemon zest from the fruit and then chop fine.) Mix in as much garlic as you like and stir or mash together with your fingertips. Hold at room temperature before serving.

PANTRY NOTE: Substitute the parsley with arugula or mint, and switch out the lemon peel for orange peel, and serve with white fish. Throw in a handful of finely chopped almonds or pine nuts for a fresh pesto.

Onion—Thyme Tart

[MAKES 1 TART]

Puff pastry is a delicate, flaky pastry made by folding layers of butter between layers of dough. I made it once (a very laborious process!), then decided that I'd rather save time and buy it from the freezer section of my local grocer. Puff is an excellent staple to keep in your frozen pantry, as it can be used for both sweet and savory dishes. I consider it my lazy food: it's quick-baking and a great shortcut for serving a crowd. Puff pastry sheets are large and take little effort to embellish. I serve this onion—thyme tart as a complement to soup or salad or for an easy predinner nibble.

> 3 tablespoons olive oil
> 2 yellow onions, cut into thin half moons
> 1 teaspoon salt
> 5 to 7 sprigs fresh thyme, leaves stripped and chopped, divided
> 1 sheet frozen puff pastry, defrosted and kept cool

Heat the olive oil in a large sauté pan over medium heat. Add the onions and stir continuously until softened, 8 to 10 minutes. Sprinkle in the salt and continue stirring. The onions will release their moisture and your sauté pan will become more and more dry, but just keep turning them every few minutes. Add half of the thyme and reduce the heat to medium low. Cook onions for about 30 to 40 minutes or more, until caramelized and golden. (If the onions start to brown and burn, reduce the heat to low.) Remove caramelized onions from the heat and set aside.

Preheat the oven to 350 degrees F. Arrange puff pastry on a parchment-lined baking sheet. Scatter the top evenly with the onions. Bake on the center oven rack for 25 to 35 minutes, until the puff is golden brown and flaky. Remove from the oven, sprinkle the remaining thyme over the top, and let cool for 10 minutes before slicing into small squares for serving.

PANTRY NOTE: Any leftover tart should be kept at room temp, lightly covered with parchment. These leftovers are best served the next day. You can crisp them up in an oven or toaster oven, but they're just as delicious served at room temp.

Panzanella Salad with Pickled Red Onions

[MAKES 4 SERVINGS]

This salad is a smart way to use up all kinds of leftovers—good for day-old bread, a glut of tomatoes in summer, or extending a small amount of salad greens. A traditional Italian dish, panzanella salad can be made with almost anything—leftover tuna, a boiled egg, mint leaves, peppers, a squeeze of lemon juice, and so on. I like the spice from pickled red onions (see the various Quick Pickle recipes in chapter 1, "Stocking the Pantry"), and I prefer to grill or broil my bread cubes until they are almost burned. That black char gives the salad a nice flavor and lends the bread a sturdy body to soak up tomato water and vinaigrette. You can omit the basil or mint—just make sure to use one or the other herb. Spicy green arugula works well with the sweet tomatoes and will hold up to the charred bread, but you can use any salad greens you prefer or have in your pantry garden.

4 cups day-old bread, cut into 1-inch cubes and grilled or broiled
    until charred
2 large heirloom tomatoes
4 tablespoons olive oil
2 tablespoons sherry vinegar
About 4 cups arugula or salad greens
¼ cup pickled red onions (prepared or store-bought)
12 basil leaves, torn
6 mint leaves, torn
Handful of olives *(optional)*
Salt and pepper

Place the grilled bread cubes in a large mixing bowl. Squeeze the tomatoes over the bowl, letting the juices drain and drip over the bread cubes (or roughly chop tomatoes on a cutting board and add tomato and juices to the bowl). Add the crushed tomato, along with the olive oil and sherry vinegar. Stir well to combine and set aside, letting the croutons soak for about 20 minutes.

When the croutons are soft but not mushy, gently mix in the arugula, pickled red onions, basil, mint, and olives. Season with salt and pepper to your liking. Serve immediately.

PANTRY NOTE: This salad holds for one day in the fridge. Cover securely and eat the next day.

Herb Storage & Drying 101

Often a recipe calling for a specific fresh herb will use only some of the packet you purchased at the grocery store. Short of growing your own garden of herbs (see chapter 9, "The Pantry Garden"), you can extend the life of herbs in numerous ways. Proper storage is key. I've had Italian parsley last somewhere near two weeks before and have kept basil fresh and lively for days. When herbs are just about on their last leg, it's best to dry and store them for later use. Fresh herbs that have been dried typically have more flavor than store-purchased, and drying and saving your herbs economizes the cost of buying them.

FRESH HERB STORAGE. Herb stems are much like flowers in that they are live plants and can be kept in water. Just as you purchase flowers and keep them in fresh water for longevity, many herbs can be treated in the same manner. Certain herbs take well to this herb-in-standing-water idea, and others keep well wrapped in a layer of slightly damp napkin or paper towel then stored in an airtight plastic bag in the fridge.

Herbs for standing water. Fresh lovage, chervil, parsley, and basil (basil will turn black when refrigerated, so always hold at room temp). Trim stems and stand the herbs in a glass filled with water to a depth of about 1 inch. Change water every other day to keep herbs fresh, trimming stems as needed.

Herbs for wrapping for the fridge. Thyme, mint, sage, rosemary, and anise hyssop.

HERB DRYING. Herbs need a warm, dry place for drying. Molds, bacteria, and yeast all thrive in moisture and can ruin herb-saving projects, so keep drying herbs free from excess moisture. There are two methods for drying herbs: hanging or tray drying. For hanging herbs, tie the stems of herbs together and hang from a hook in your ceiling until dry. For tray drying, place herbs on a parchment-lined baking sheet (turn them occasionally so moisture does not collect under the leaves). Most herbs should dry out in four to six days. They are fully dry when they crumble easily to the touch. Once herbs are dry, crumble the leaves into a glass jar and store in your spice cupboard (which should be cool, dry, and far from any heat sources).

SAVING SEEDS. Some herbs are saved for their seed, such as dill, parsley, and coriander. In that case, once dry, shake the stalk of the herb over a paper bag and the seeds will collect at the bottom. Fennel pollen can be collected in the same fashion once it flowers in midsummer. Store seeds as you would dried leaves—in small glass spice jars.

chapter 3

whole grains

WHEN I WAS A LITTLE GIRL, my mom would occasionally make beef and barley soup. I distinctly remember the cracked grain of barley, fluffy and floating in the fat-speckled broth, and the chewiness of the grain as I held it between my two front teeth and made a game of trying to split it in half. For some reason I wanted to bite the barley with the front of my mouth, to really feel the texture, as opposed to using my little molars to chew. My mom's soup was heavy with oil, no doubt from the beef, and the barley actually didn't taste like much, but the meat was fatty and juicy. Overall each spoonful was intensely satisfying. Although my mom didn't make beef and barley soup often, it left an impression and fueled an obsession that I picked up as an adult.

Whole grains are actual plant seeds. They are an excellent source of fiber and often protein. Whole grains are slowly metabolized by the body, leaving us feeling satisfied longer and contributing to stabilized blood sugar levels. This sounds terribly scientific, but there are important facts to consider when choosing whole grains. It is widely accepted that whole grains are paramount to a healthy diet and aid in the prevention of cancer, heart disease, and diabetes. There is no doubt about the health benefits of adding whole grains to your diet, but the trick is to make sure they taste good too.

When working with a new ingredient such as a whole grain, my advice is to start small and stay focused. Choose one or two grains that sound appealing and then begin exploring. Back in the kitchen, steam a batch to get the full flavor of the grain without embellishment. Steamed or boiled grain that has been cooked with nothing but water and a pinch of salt is a bit boring, but boring isn't always bad. For the most part, however, whole grains need some doctoring up and flavor-layering to really make them sing. There are a few ways to go about this:

1. ADD FAT. Everything, as they say, tastes better with butter, particularly in the realm of dried whole grains. And bacon. And cheese. Plain polenta turns absolutely velvety with just a spoonful of butter and a pinch of salt mixed in. Same goes for most whole grains. Fats include butter, cheese, olive oil, nut oils, crème fraîche, and so on. You could also use plain yogurt (nonfat and full fat work equally well in almost any recipe).

2. FLAVOR YOUR COOKING WATER. In other words, cook with stock. You can easily add flavor and complexity to a dish by cooking with stock, whether chicken, vegetable, or beef. Or you could flavor the cooking water with "aromatics," which is a fancy way of saying spices-that-give-off-flavor. Think citrus peels, dried spices, or fresh herbs.

3. VARY THE TECHNIQUE. Steamed whole grains can be used in a handful of clever fashions. Steamed, they can provide the base for stuffing baked mushrooms or peppers. Those same grains can be crisp-cooked, as you would a potato, in a sauté pan with garlic and oil over high heat. Serve these crispy grains as a side dish to grilled meat. Plainly steamed grains may also be baked with milk and a beaten egg—sort of like if custard and rice pudding had a baby. To overuse a phrase, think outside the box and be flexible.

For pantry stocking your whole grains, I recommend buying from bulk bins for several reasons. First, it is possible for whole grains to go rancid (although this typically happens to grains that have been pressed to flakes or ground into flour). Be sure to eat these grains and flours within three months of purchasing or store them airtight in the fridge. Second, buying from bulk bins allows you the freedom to work with different grains without too much of an investment. There is nothing worse than jars of ingredients sitting in a cupboard, going unused. Instead, purchase in small quantities that can be easily worked through. In this chapter I've provided a variety of recipes using whole grains at breakfast, lunch, dinner, dessert, and snack time. Instead of focusing on the plethora of whole grains, I highlight four grains that are readily available to the home cook and easy to work with.

BARLEY. My childhood favorite, barley is typically available in pressed flakes, whole grains, milled flour, and pearled versions. Whole barley does better if you give it a soak before using, both because that will speed up what is certain to be a long cooking process and because it helps to make nutrients more available to our digestive systems. Barley can be used in sweets (as a flour), as a hearty addition to soups and salads, and as a sautéed side dish. Pearled barley has been refined—its outer bran buffed off—and can be used for risotto, which I make year-round by changing out the vegetable additions to suit the season. It's important to note that whole barley will not absorb liquid as pearled barley will, so you cannot use that version for risotto. For more fiber in your diet, look for a bran-flecked pearled barley when purchasing, not the all-white versions that don't contain bran.

BULGUR. Easy to prepare, bulgur requires no real cooking. You need only boil water and let it steep into the grain. Use steamed bulgur as a base for a healthy and light meal. Bulgur is the product of wheat berries that have been steamed and dried, then broken down to a coarse grain of varying size. Rely on it for healthful salads, with rotating ingredients from the pantry. It is a staple in Middle Eastern recipes, so I look to them for kitchen inspiration. My Turkish friend Aliye steams and seasons bulgur, then uses it as a stuffing in rolled-up chard leaves or bell peppers (see "Stuffings: Savory Fillings" in chapter 1, "Stocking the Pantry"). Bulgur is used in the popular dish tabbouleh—a mix of tomato, herb, and lemon juice at its simplest. Opt for bulgur over white rice or couscous for its higher nutritional qualities.

FARRO. Farro is the rock star grain of the group. Little known outside of Italy, farro is just now being grown domestically by a small handful of family farms. Also known as emmer, farro was introduced stateside by restaurants and has since started to find its way to the kitchen of many home cooks. Farro is worth sourcing online or keeping an eye out for at the farmers market. Farro is nutty and firm, like barley, but the grain is softer and more refined. It is excellent as a ground flour used in baked goods or handmade pasta. It does not have a strong nutty aroma (as whole wheat and barley flours tend to), so it does not overpower sweets.

QUINOA. A mild-flavored, protein-packed grain, quinoa has grown in popularity over the past few years and is now widely available. It has a great texture because its germ (the outer hull) breaks from the seed. The germ remains as a ring of crunchy texture encasing the soft and tender seed. This sounds a bit odd, but it looks beautiful and is fascinating to observe. Also of note, quinoa is gluten-free, as it is not a member of the wheat family. It is considered a "grain" but in fact is an herbaceous flowering plant. Quinoa can be prepared in many ways—both sweet and savory recipes work well with it.

whole grains
{ RECIPES }

Hippie Hotcakes
[MAKES 2 SERVINGS]

The first time I made these pancakes for my friend Patric (a trained pastry chef), he took one look at the plate and said, "What the hell are these? Some sort of hippie pancakes?" Just like that, a recipe was born. Not your traditional fluffy breakfast pancakes, these hotcakes are flat and thin. Made with soaked grains, not flour, they make a healthful and easy breakfast. Soak the grains overnight and then whiz everything up in the blender the next morning. Because the batter is so loose, use a small frying pan for these if you have one; otherwise the hotcakes will spread a bit wider than you might prefer.

½ cup steel-cut oats

½ cup quinoa, washed and rinsed three times (until the water runs clear)

½ cup plain yogurt (nonfat or full fat is fine)

1 cup water

1 teaspoon sugar

¼ teaspoon salt

½ teaspoon cinnamon

½ teaspoon freshly grated nutmeg

3 eggs

1 teaspoon baking powder

2 tablespoons coconut oil, melted (or 2 tablespoons unsalted butter),
    plus more for pan

Put the steel-cut oats, quinoa, yogurt, and water in a blender, cover, and refrigerate overnight. In the morning, add the remaining ingredients. Cover then blend on low to incorporate, at least 1 minute. Move the setting to purée or liquefy and blend 1 minute more, until the hotcake batter is smooth.

Heat a scoop of coconut oil in a small skillet over medium heat. When the skillet is hot, pour in some batter until it reaches the edges (about ½ cup for one large pancake), and cook for 3 or 4 minutes, until golden brown and bubbles on the surface are popped. Flip the hotcake and cook the other side for another 3 or 4 minutes, until brown and cooked through. Serve with Berry Syrup (in chapter 1, "Stocking the Pantry") or traditional maple syrup.

PANTRY NOTE: Quinoa is gluten-free, and some gluten-intolerant people are able to digest steel-cut oats easily. Do your homework on your breakfast guests: use all quinoa in this recipe or substitute buckwheat groats (which are a fruit, not a grain) for a totally gluten-free breakfast. Leftover hotcakes can be cooled, then kept in a plastic or produce bag in the freezer for four to six weeks. When reheating the hotcakes, pop them in a toaster or under the broiler for a few minutes on each side.

Breakfast Grains

Here is a simple and savvy idea for using extra grains. First and foremost, make sure that you don't season grains when you steam them. If you know you're going to make a pot of savory barley for a side dish to your chicken, for example, do not add an onion and make the whole pot of grains savory—just steam it plain and add your flavors later. This is an expert tip because inevitably you'll have leftovers. If all those leftovers are scented with onion and herb, you'll have to use them in another savory way. If, however, they are left simple, you have an opportunity to make an entirely new dish by adding other ingredients.

Any grain works in this easy Breakfast Grains recipe—brown rice, barley, bulgur, and so on. Put a handful of already-steamed grains in a bowl. (I don't heat up the grains because I'm too lazy and I only want to use one pot.) Add flavor—some vanilla sugar or a sprinkle of ground cinnamon or freshly grated nutmeg. Over medium-low heat, bring 1 cup of milk (per serving) to a simmer. (I make sure to warm a little extra for my coffee.) When heated, pour your milk over the cold grains and eat straightaway.

Barley & Sweet Potato Salad

[MAKES 6 TO 8 SIDE-DISH SERVINGS]

This dish rocks. It is truly delicious—my idea of food heaven. Healthy grains + fresh herbs + olive oil = perfection. If you're feeling lazy and don't want to pop to the shop for a sweet potato, you can skip it (although the salad is much better with it). The little cubes of crispy sweet potatoes are addictive. This is a great picnic salad, packed in a container for a day trip, or brought over to a friend's barbeque as a side dish. Any leftovers will keep well in the fridge for several days without getting mushy or losing their flavor.

> 1 cup uncooked barley
> 3 cups water
> Pinch of salt
> 1½ tablespoons coconut oil
> 1 sweet potato, peeled and diced into small cubes
> Salt and pepper
> ¼ cup chopped fresh tender herbs (a mixture of parsley, chive,
>   anise hyssop, basil, or lovage)
> 3 tablespoons olive oil
> 2 tablespoons champagne vinegar (or a squeeze of lemon)

Place saucepan over medium-high heat. Add dry barley and toast until fragrant, 3 to 5 minutes, stirring often. Add water and bring the mixture to a boil over high heat, then reduce to a simmer and cook for 50 to 60 minutes, until tender but al dente. Drain any leftover liquid, cool to room temperature, and set aside.

While the barley is cooking, heat the coconut oil in a sauté pan over medium heat. When the oil is hot and showing ripples, place a single layer of the sweet potato cubes in the pan and sprinkle with salt. Cook, stirring only occasionally, until all sides are golden brown, about 7 to 10 minutes.

In a serving bowl, gently mix together the sweet potato fries and the barley. Stir in the fresh herbs, olive oil, and champagne vinegar. Season with salt and pepper to taste. Adjust the olive oil and herbs to your liking. Serve at room temperature.

PANTRY NOTE: This salad will hold for five days in the fridge, in an airtight container. If you make extra barley, set some aside so you can store it in a plastic bag in the freezer. Toss the frozen grains into warmed milk for an easy weekday breakfast. If you don't have coconut oil, use olive oil to fry the potatoes.

Pearled Barley Risotto with Sherried Mushrooms & Leeks

[MAKES 4 SERVINGS]

I love risotto but have often steered clear of the dish, as it's made with traditional arborio rice, which doesn't have a lot of fiber. I heard about someone using barley for risotto years ago and a lightbulb went off in my head. With pearled barley, you get more fiber in each serving, and the grain is lower in calories. Can't be beat! Also, contrary to culinary lore, you do not need to hover over your pot and stir the living daylights out of risotto. I am careful to give it a stir every few minutes, but I don't watch it with an eagle eye, and it has always come out perfectly. For this recipe I prep the mushrooms and leeks on the side and add them to the finished pot of risotto just before serving.

Olive oil

1 cup chopped onion

1 cup uncooked pearled barley

4 to 5 cups chicken or vegetable stock or water,
    warmed and held over low heat, divided

1 leek, washed of grit and sliced into thin ribbons

2 cups button mushrooms, whole if small or chopped if large

Salt and pepper

2 tablespoons sherry or marsala

Cover the bottom of a 5-quart stockpot with a thin layer of olive oil and heat over medium-high. When heated, cook and stir the onion until soft, about 5 to 6 minutes. Add the pearled barley and cook until starting to brown, about 2 minutes more. Pour in 1 cup of the chicken stock and reduce the heat to medium/medium-low. Stir the barley–onion mixture until all the liquid is incorporated. Add another cup of the stock. Continue stirring and adding stock in this fashion, 1 cup at a time, until the barley is cooked al dente, about 40 minutes. Note that cooking time can take anywhere from 30 to 45 minutes, depending on the moisture content, germ thickness, and age of the barley.

While the barley is cooking, prep the vegetables. Heat 2 tablespoons olive oil in a sauté pan over medium heat. Cook and stir the leek until softened, about 5 minutes. Add as many mushrooms as can fit in the pan and season with a few pinches of salt. Cook the mushrooms down, stirring occasionally, and add the rest in batches by the handful until all the mushrooms are incorporated. When they stop releasing moisture, turn the heat to medium-high and stir continuously.

When the pan seems dry and the mushroom–leek mixture begins to brown and stick, pour in the sherry to deglaze the pan. Scrape up any brown bits and cook for another minute, then remove the mixture from the heat and set aside.

When the risotto is al dente, stir the mushroom–leek mixture into the stockpot. Season with salt and pepper to your liking. Serve and, if desired, garnish with freshly grated Parmesan and chopped fresh parsley.

PANTRY NOTE: Barley risotto will keep, covered in the fridge, for three to four days. Refresh flavor by adding fresh parsley to leftovers. Barley risotto can be served at room temp.

Spiced Kibbe

[MAKES 2 SERVINGS]

Kibbe is a Middle Eastern dish that uses meat and bulgur as the main components. For me, it is the perfect meal solution, as it combines protein-rich and belly-satisfying ground meat with nutrient-rich grains. This Arab-inspired dish is a great way to extend expensive grain-fed meat to feed more mouths. My version is pretty stripped down and simple, but at its core kibbe is a spice-heavy and fragrant dish that can be prepped and cooked in less than 30 minutes. Herby Yogurt (in chapter 7, "Milk & Yogurt") is a cooling side that adds some healthy fat to the lean proteins in the kibbe, but plain yogurt is equally delicious.

> ³/₄ cup uncooked bulgur
> 1¹/₂ cups boiling water (plus a smidge more)
> 1 cup (about 8 ounces or ¹/₂ pound) ground beef or lamb
> 1 teaspoon garam masala
> ¹/₂ teaspoon salt
> ¹/₂ teaspoon red chile flakes
> ¹/₂ teaspoon ground cinnamon
> 1 teaspoon dried mint, oregano, or dill
> Freshly ground black pepper
> Olive oil

Put the bulgur in a medium-sized glass bowl and pour in the boiling water. Cover the bowl with plastic wrap or a plate and set aside to steam until the water is absorbed and grains are al dente, about 20 to 25 minutes. Drain any additional water from the grains, and cool.

In a large mixing bowl, use your hands to combine the ground beef, bulgur, and all the spices. When the mixture is well-combined, form 6 small, equally proportioned patties and set aside.

Heat olive oil in a sauté pan over medium heat. Cook the kibbe patties until golden brown, 4 to 5 minutes per side. Remove from the heat and serve immediately.

PANTRY NOTE: Kibbe freezes very well, so double up on the recipe and freeze some extra patties. Warm up frozen patties in a toaster oven or under the broiler.

Bulgur & Citrus Salad

[MAKES 4 SERVINGS]

Bulgur is like the gateway drug for whole grains, as it is commonly available and simple to make. You've likely had bulgur in a traditional salad: tabbouleh. When I first started making tabbouleh at home, I burned myself out and grew tired of the same old preparation. Then one day I had my friend Lynda's bulgur salad. She used the outer peel and juice of an orange as the vinaigrette and that bright sweet-citrusy pop was the perfect acid to wake up these grains.

You can substitute one fresh herb for another, but don't forgo using them, as the herbs really contribute to the success of this salad. I don't specify the quantity for the dried fruit—it's up to you how much you'd like to add, if any. Some days I want a fruity mouthful in each bite; other days I only want the sweetness every third bite or so.

1 cup uncooked bulgur

1½ cups boiling water (plus a smidge more)

¼ cup pine nuts, toasted

¼ cup chopped fresh parsley

¼ cup chopped fresh mint

¼ teaspoon ground cinnamon

Handful of dried currants or raisins

Half an orange, grated outer peel and juice only

1 teaspoon red wine vinegar

Olive oil

Salt and pepper

Put the bulgur in a medium-sized glass bowl and pour in the boiling water. Cover the bowl with plastic wrap or a plate and set aside to steam until all the water is absorbed and grain is al dente, about 20 to 25 minutes. Drain any additional water from the grains.

Stir in the pine nuts, parsley, mint, cinnamon, and dried fruit. Add the orange peel, orange juice, and vinegar, drizzle with olive oil, and mix gently. Season with salt and pepper to taste. Serve at room temp.

PANTRY NOTE: You can toast pine nuts easily in a dry sauté pan set over medium-high heat. Stir frequently until brown, about 5 minutes. This salad can be made in advance and stored in the fridge for up to four days. It easily transitions to a stuffing for zucchini, chard leaves, peppers, and tomatoes (see "Stuffing: Savory Fillings" in chapter 1, "Stocking the Pantry").

Anise-Farro Biscotti

[MAKES 2 DOZEN]

I used to make this recipe with barley flour, as I'm always after a healthier version of the foods I love. I won't feel nearly as guilty eating cookies if I've made them with the protein-dense, complex carbohydrates found in whole grains. Emmer flour, or farro as it's sometimes called, is an ancient grain that Italians have been using for centuries. I like to use this low-gluten flour when I'm trying to make a crisp or crumbly cookie.

I have to admit that these cookies never come out the way I want them to, insofar as shape and look, but they taste fantastic! Don't fuss over getting the dough shaped just right. Let it land how it lands on your baking sheet, push it around as best you can, and call it done—otherwise you'll drive yourself crazy shooting for perfection. Trust me. Real tooth-breakers, these biscotti are best dunked, served with espresso or a big cup of tea.

> 3 eggs
> Half a lemon, grated outer peel and about 2 tablespoons juice only
> 1 tablespoon vanilla extract
> 1 teaspoon anise oil
> 2 1/4 cups emmer flour
> 1 cup brown sugar
> 1 teaspoon baking soda
> 2 pinches of salt
> 2 tablespoons anise seed

Preheat the oven to 350 degrees F.

Using an electric mixer, combine the eggs, lemon peel and juice, vanilla extract, and anise oil. On medium speed, add the emmer flour, brown sugar, baking soda, salt, and anise seed until everything is well incorporated. Let the dough stand for 5 or 10 minutes.

Line a baking sheet with parchment paper or grease it with a bit of olive oil. Using a bread scraper or a large rubber spatula, scoop out half of the batter and drop onto the baking sheet. Shape the dough into a rectangular log, about 3 to 4 inches wide. Do the same with the remaining dough, using a second baking sheet if needed.

Bake on the center rack for 30 minutes. Remove the baking sheet from the oven and reduce the oven temperature to 300 degrees F. Slice the dough into wedges of biscotti, about $1/4$-inch to $3/4$-inch thick, depending on your preference. Place the biscotti wedges cut side down on the baking sheet and bake for another 10 to 15 minutes, until golden brown. Remove from the oven and cool.

PANTRY NOTE: You can substitute almond oil for the anise oil, but cut the measurement to $1/2$ teaspoon. It's okay to omit the anise seed. Store biscotti in an airtight container for up to a week (or until they turn stale), or freeze baked cookies in a resealable plastic bag, defrosting prior to serving.

Vanilla Quinoa Pudding

[MAKES 4 TO 6 SERVINGS]

I love the flavor in a rich cinnamon-scented rice pudding, but I don't love white rice. Not nutrient-dense enough for me. Instead, I use quinoa, which is a soft grain that works beautifully. It is super important that you wash your quinoa before you cook it. Because I like taking shortcuts, I learned this the hard way the first time I worked with this grain. I did not wash it, and I ruined what could've been a perfectly delicious dessert with a bitter and unappetizing flavor. It was so awful that I have not made the same mistake twice. Wash the quinoa in a big bowl of water by rubbing the grains between your fingertips or the palm of your hand. Three changes of water typically gets the grain clean. When the water runs clear, you're set.

> 1 cup quinoa, washed and rinsed well
> 3 cups whole milk
> 1 fresh vanilla bean, split, beans scraped into pot
> ¼ cup raisins
> ½ cup sugar
> 1 cinnamon stick

In a large saucepot, heat all of the ingredients over medium heat. Bring the mixture to a soft boil, then cover and reduce to low. Cook until most of the liquid is absorbed, about 30 minutes, stirring occasionally. (There will be a pool of milk at the bottom of the pot, but don't worry about that.)

Remove the quinoa mixture from the heat and, with the lid on, set aside for another 20 to 30 minutes, until all the liquid is absorbed. Serve warm and garnish with a sprinkle of cinnamon and a bit of cold heavy cream, if you like.

PANTRY NOTE: Chocolate shavings as garnish fancy up this otherwise homey dessert. Because it's a bit laborious to wash quinoa, I typically measure out twice what this recipe calls for and I steam the other cup of quinoa for another use later in the week. The plain steamed quinoa will hold in the fridge for about five days. Like most grains, cooked quinoa will also freeze well.

chapter 4

beans & peas

ONE OF THE GOALS IN STOCKING a pantry is to balance the contents perfectly so all ingredients are used in a timely fashion. You don't want to stock too many perishable items at the same time—that means you have to *eat* them at the same time. Fresh produce in the pantry is the most susceptible to spoilage, quickly followed by dairy. From there, nuts and whole grains may turn rancid in time. Yet through all these cycles of food in and out of the pantry, legumes are an ever constant staple. It is rare that a dried bean will go bad. Beans have a long shelf life and don't often suffer from spoilage, although aged beans may take longer to cook. They also offer a measure of health that few other pantry items can claim. Rich in protein and high in fiber, beans act as hearty sustenance. Outside of meat, legumes offer a level of nutrition that not many other foods can. They are made up of mostly complex carbohydrates and are an excellent source of iron. They store well and are relatively inexpensive. Legumes are considered a superfood—one that promotes health and aids in disease prevention.

Beans have been cultivated for centuries and are available in many varieties. Dried beans and peas are in fact the seeds from the plant. People are always amazed when they see beans being planted, as they look no different from the dried beans we eat. There are broad beans, more commonly known as favas; runner beans; fat plump beans like coronas or cannellinis; and common beans, navy beans, shelling peas, and pintos. Beans can be mealy with a chewy skin or thin-skinned and buttery, depending on the variety. For the pantry, I vastly prefer dried beans over canned beans, as they allow a home cook to have absolute control over salt and flavor. Dried beans also have better texture than canned beans that have been sitting in water (although in a pinch canned beans will work). Purchase dried beans from the bulk bins when you can, and opt for small amounts. Keep in mind that one cup of dried beans can serve four people.

Dried beans do well with a proper soaking before cooking. Typically, setting them out on the counter overnight gives them enough time to soften and helps to break down the simple sugars in legumes that we cannot fully digest. After soaking beans, it is imperative to discard the soaking liquid and use fresh water for cooking them. Many cultures cook beans along with cumin and coriander to aid in digestion. Small legumes such as lentils do not need to soak, as they cook quickly.

Legumes can be served as room-temperature salads, simmered in broth for soup and stews, or cooked in water to make a simple pot of beans. Beans take well to flavor, and need a heavy salting during cooking. I don't subscribe to the idea that salting beans during cooking makes them tougher. I have always found a generous salting makes them taste better in the end. Cooking times vary depending on the bean, so it's best left to the cook to decide when the beans are ready. Bean dishes are one of those meals best served the next day. As they have time to take in flavor, beans taste better after cooking and resting a bit. Although beans are lovely cooked simply in water, flavor can be added by cooking in vegetable or chicken stock or by using aromatics in the broth. I vacillate between cooking beans covered and uncovered. There is no noticeable difference, although uncovered beans should be checked for adequate liquid as they cook, adding some when necessary.

Cannellini beans (a medium-sized white runner bean), black beans, chickpeas, French lentils (the shiny black variety), and navy beans are my beans of choice for the pantry. These varieties are widely available, and each offers a different range of size, texture, and taste. Heirloom beans, however, have been cropping up in recent years and should definitely be tried for a break from the norm. They are often gorgeously colored, and by using rare beans, you can help preserve seed diversity in our food system *and* in your pantry.

beans & peas
{ RECIPES }

Herbal Minestrone

[MAKES 4 TO 6 SERVINGS]

Always on a mission to use any leftovers, I find minestrone soup is the perfect dish for adding a little bit of this and a little bit of that. Minestrone is an Italian country soup that typically contains beans or pasta, along with any vegetables in season. The secret to this recipe's success lies in not overcooking the vegetables. Adding them in the last 15 minutes of cooking ensures they will keep their shape and not break down, making this more of an herby soup than a stew. If you like, garnish with a float of olive oil and freshly grated Parmesan for a rich sharpness.

Olive oil
1/2 onion, chopped, plus 1/2 cup finely diced onion
1 cup dried broad beans or other large bean, soaked overnight
    and drained
5 cups chicken or vegetable stock
1 tablespoon salt
Salt and pepper
1/2 cup peeled and chopped carrot
1/2 cup chopped zucchini
2 cups leftover cooked pasta
1/2 cup roughly chopped fresh Italian parsley (about half a bunch)
1/2 cup roughly chopped fresh mint (leaves from about 7 sprigs)

Cover the bottom of a large stockpot with a layer of olive oil and set over medium heat. When hot, add the chopped half onion, cooking and stirring until soft, about 5 to 7 minutes. Add the beans and chicken stock and bring to a boil. Stir in the salt.

Reduce the heat to medium-low, and simmer until the beans are soft and can be mashed easily with the back of a spoon, about 2 to 4 hours. (Cooking time depends on the bean and varies widely.) Season with salt and pepper to taste.

When the beans are soft, stir in the carrot and the finely diced onion. Cook for about 10 minutes, then add zucchini until just cooked, another 5 minutes or so. When the veggies are cooked through but still toothsome, add the leftover pasta, parsley, and mint. Serve immediately.

PANTRY NOTE: This soup is a great way to use up any leftover pasta, which is otherwise not very tasty. Cut long noodles into small pieces, or leave them whole. If you don't have any leftover pasta, it is fine to omit it or make a bit on the side for the soup.

Apricot-Chickpea Salad

[MAKES 6 TO 8 SERVINGS]

I prefer to use dried chickpeas (also known as garbanzo beans) in this recipe. I soak them for a few hours before boiling with salt and water until tender. They retain a nice bite, and I find canned peas a bit too soft. But use whichever you prefer, as the flavors in this salad are really the star. A blend of dried fruit and herbs creates a very flavorful dish. The vinaigrette is a simple dressing of olive oil, red wine vinegar, Dijon mustard, herbs, and spices—all pantry basics.

3 cups dried chickpeas, soaked and drained

Salt

Half bunch of Italian parsley, stemmed and chopped

1/2 cup dried Turkish apricots, sliced into thin slivers

10 to 12 kalamata olives, pitted and coarsely chopped

VINAIGRETTE

1/4 cup olive oil

1/4 cup red wine vinegar

1 tablespoon Dijon mustard

1 clove garlic, minced

1 teaspoon ground paprika

2 teaspoons chopped fresh oregano (or 1 teaspoon dried)

2 teaspoons chopped fresh marjoram (or 1 teaspoon dried)

1/2 teaspoon salt

1/2 teaspoon red chile flakes

Drain chickpeas, place in a large saucepan, and cover with water. Add a healthy pinch of salt and bring to a boil. Reduce to a simmer and cook until tender, 40 to 60 minutes. Drain and cool.

In a small bowl, whisk together all vinaigrette ingredients. Put the cooled chickpeas in a large serving bowl and cover with the dressing. Stir to combine, then mix in the parsley, apricots, and olives. Let the salad stand at least 2 hours before serving.

PANTRY NOTE: This salad will keep for several days, in an airtight container, in the fridge. Refresh by adding fresh herbs before serving leftovers.

Vinaigrette

Vinaigrettes and dressings are simple to make and have the ability to instantly change a salad or meal. At its core, vinaigrette is a mix of oil and acid. From that base, flavors can be added and layered—either subtly or full-on. Three parts oil to one part acid and you're set. Although a simple drizzle of olive oil with a squeeze of fresh lemon juice and a pinch of salt and pepper should definitely not be overlooked, the options for vinaigrettes are truly infinite.

The fat, or oil, in a vinaigrette can be replaced with other rich ingredients—nut oils (like sesame or walnut), eggs (either raw or hard-boiled and mashed), or a smashed-up avocado. The acid can be altered slightly by changing the citrus from lemon to orange or lime juice. You can also try a bevy of vinegars (rice wine vinegar, sherry vinegar, apple cider vinegar), or think creatively and use pickling juice from your preserves. Traditional vinaigrette is made with Dijon mustard, although you can add flavors simply by including a handful of chopped herbs, some fresh grated ginger, or chopped shallots. A little sweetness in a vinaigrette mellows out the acidity and softens the flavor. Try adding a teaspoon of honey, some fruit syrup from your canned preserves, or molasses.

While vinaigrettes are naturals for lettuces and room-temp grains or legumes, vinaigrettes need not be relegated only to salads. Used as a finishing component to fish or meat or as a finish to sauces, vinaigrettes have the tendency to brighten a dish. They can be brushed on just-done fish, which benefits from acid to engage the palate. With thick cuts of meat (like a pork shoulder or a thick-cut steak) vinaigrettes can be used as marinades, with the acid helping to tenderize the meat.

EVERYDAY VINAIGRETTE
3 tablespoons olive oil
1 tablespoon red wine vinegar
1 teaspoon Dijon mustard
Salt and pepper

Lentils with Mint & Beets

[MAKES 4 TO 6 SERVINGS]

Lentils are pretty much a superfood. High in protein and fiber, they cook more quickly than other legumes and can be used in salads, soups, and as hearty side dishes. They are infinitely flexible, although I like them best in come-together-easily room-temperature salads. This version has pretty red beets for both color and flavor, and ribbons of mint for some liveliness. I serve it in winter, summer, and any season in between. It's also a great dish to make for crowds, as lentils are quite inexpensive. Opt for the tiny black French lentils for this recipe; they hold their shape the best.

Olive oil

1 clove garlic, chopped

½ medium red onion, finely chopped

1 cup dried French lentils

1 teaspoon salt

3 medium beets, tops removed and scrubbed of any dirt

15 fresh mint leaves

VINAIGRETTE

4 tablespoons olive oil

2 tablespoons red wine vinegar

1 teaspoon Dijon mustard

Good pinch of salt

Freshly ground black pepper

Cover the bottom of a medium saucepan with olive oil and heat over medium-high. Cook and stir the onion and garlic for 5 to 7 minutes, or until soft. Add the French lentils, salt, and enough water so that the lentils are just covered. Bring to a boil, reduce the heat to medium-low, and cover and simmer until the lentils are cooked but still have bite, about 20 to 25 minutes. Drain any excess water and pour the cooked lentils onto a sheet pan to cool quickly and halt the cooking process.

Meanwhile, bring a small pot of water to boil and cook the whole beets until soft (time will vary depending on the size of the beet, so check every 20 minutes or so). Cool the beets slightly, rub off the skin with a paper towel (it will peel away easily), and chop the beets into small cubes. Chiffonade the mint leaves by stacking whole leaves and rolling them up lengthwise. When you have a tight roll, cut into thin ribbons.

To prepare the vinaigrette, pour the olive oil, red wine vinegar, Dijon mustard, and salt into a small jar, cover, and shake to combine. Season with salt and pepper as you like.

In a large serving bowl, combine the cooled lentils, beets, and vinaigrette. Gently fold in the mint leaves (reserve a few for garnish). Serve at room temperature.

PANTRY NOTE: This dish will hold for five days in the fridge and does not freeze well. This salad is also excellent with a few spoonfuls of chèvre, some toasted walnuts—or both!

Peanut Soba Noodles

[MAKES 4 SERVINGS]

I love Asian food and have a well-stocked Asian pantry full of rice wine vinegar, fish sauce, chili paste, soy sauce, and sesame oil—pretty much the cornerstone ingredients to an easy and fragrant meal. When I'm in a hurry, I quickly boil some soba noodles, which are traditionally made with buckwheat flour—a great gluten-free source of protein. (Buckwheat is a flower, not a grain.) This peanut sauce can be made thicker by adding more peanut butter or thinner by adding more water. The fish sauce isn't necessary but will give the peanut sauce an incomparable depth of flavor. Bet you thought peanuts were a nut. They are not—they are actually a legume!

PEANUT SAUCE
1/2 cup peanut butter
1/4 cup water
1/4 cup soy sauce
Half a lime, juice only
1 clove garlic, minced
2 tablespoons rice wine vinegar
1 tablespoon fish sauce
1/2 teaspoon sesame oil

One 8-ounce package soba noodles
1 carrot, peeled and grated
Handful fresh bean sprouts
3 green onions, chopped

To prepare the peanut sauce, mix the peanut butter, water, soy sauce, lime juice, garlic, rice wine vinegar, fish sauce, and sesame oil until smooth and creamy. Set aside.

Prepare the soba noodles as directed on the package. Drain well and put the noodles in a medium-sized bowl. Toss the noodles with the peanut sauce, adding a little at a time until you are satisfied with how the noodles are dressed. Fold in the carrots, bean sprouts, and green onions.

Serve in shallow bowls with chopped cilantro and peanuts as garnish, if desired. Serve at room temperature.

PANTRY NOTE: I prefer all-natural, no-salt-added peanut butter in this recipe. You can leave out or add just about any vegetables to this salad. This dish holds for a few days in the fridge. Any leftover peanut sauce can be stored in a plastic container or glass jar and will keep for about two weeks in the fridge. Leftover sauce can be tossed with some finely chopped cabbage and toasted sesame seeds for a cold salad.

White Bean & Preserved Lemon Salad

[MAKES 4 TO 6 SERVINGS]

This is a perfect summer salad—cool beans, lemony citrus, and some heat from chile-soaked shrimp. White navy beans cook quickly and are a nice creamy bean. Because this is a salad, ideally you want to cook the beans through without breaking them down. (Otherwise you'll be stuck with beans better fit for stew.) The trick is to pull the beans from the heat as soon as they are just cooked through and continue steaming them off the heat for a bit. From there, spread them on a sheet pan, which speeds up the cooling process. Tofu can be substituted for the shrimp in this recipe, but be sure to use one or the other, as the marinade provides a spicy bite to the dish.

2 cups dried white navy beans, soaked overnight

2 tablespoons salt

¼ cup red onion, finely chopped

¼ cup fresh lovage or celery leaves, chopped

2 celery stalks, from the heart, sliced thin

1 lemon, grated outer peel and juice

1 teaspoon ground smoked paprika (or traditional paprika)

4 tablespoons olive oil

MARINADE

1 tablespoon red chile flakes

1 tablespoon preserved lemon, chopped fine (or grated outer peel
    from 1 lemon)

1 teaspoon coriander, crushed or freshly ground

1 teaspoon sumac (optional)

¼ cup olive oil

1½ pounds shrimp, peeled

In a large stockpot, cover the white navy beans with 1½ inches of water and bring to a boil. Reduce the heat to medium-low, add the salt, and simmer until the beans are just tender, about 1 hour. Remove from the heat and set aside, covered, to steam the beans until soft and creamy, another 15 to 30 minutes. Check the texture of the beans every 10 minutes (be sure not to overcook and break them down). When the beans are creamy and tender, drain any excess water and cool them completely by spreading on a sheet pan in a single layer. When cooled, place them in a large bowl and add the red onion, lovage leaves, celery, grated lemon peel and juice, paprika, and olive oil. Stir to combine. Season with salt and pepper as desired. Cover with a plate or plastic wrap and refrigerate until ready to serve.

To prepare the marinade, combine the red chile flakes, preserved lemon, coriander, sumac, and olive oil in a medium-sized bowl. Add the shrimp and let marinate for 30 minutes or up to 1 hour. Skewer the shrimp and arrange on a broiler pan. Broil the shrimp until cooked through and red chile flakes are toasted, about 4 minutes on each side.

To serve, fill small bowls with the bean salad, and top with a few pieces of shrimp. If desired, drizzle with olive oil and chopped fresh parsley for garnish.

PANTRY NOTE: This salad will keep in your fridge for about five days. Sumac is a dried and ground berry from a Middle Eastern shrub. It has a tangy taste and citrus undertone that cannot be easily replicated with other spices. You can find it in some bulk herb sections, or it can be ordered online. Preserved lemons can be made or purchased in the Middle Eastern food section at some grocery stores. Smoked paprika is a specialty food item. Substitutions have been given in the ingredients list.

Preserved Lemons

Salt has long been a means of food preservation. When this concept is applied to simple lemons, the outcome is an intensely flavored pantry ingredient that is simple to make and stores well. Lemons are sliced and rubbed with coarse salt, the juice and salt acting as the preservative. Over a few weeks the lemon rinds, pulp, and pith become soft and velvety and can be chopped and sliced for salads, relishes, stews, and more.

Preserved lemons are a staple of Moroccan cuisine but can be used in most savory dishes calling for lemon. Tasting of muted lemon, with none of the sour tang, they add a subtle undertone to dishes. Replace the fresh zest in Gremolata (see recipe in chapter 2, "Kitchen Economy") with preserved lemon, and you'll instantly change the dish. Preserved lemons have a flavor unto themselves, at once clean yet rich. They can be added to a compound butter (see the sidebar in chapter 7, "Milk & Yogurt") or used in long braises. They also add a nice flavor note to room-temperature salads, like Apricot–Chickpea Salad (see recipe in this chapter), and can be used as a quick garnish to simply steamed vegetables.

Rinse preserved lemons thoroughly in cold water before using. You must rinse off the salt, leaving behind only the sweet skin. You can scrape out the pulp and pith and finely chop or thinly slice the skins. It is also safe to use the entire lemon, but that is best used in stews or roasts. Be sure to adjust the salt in your recipe accordingly, as the preserved fruits will give off some salt.

To make preserved lemons yourself, you can use regular lemons or Meyer lemons when they are in season (in winter). Cut off the blossom end of the lemon. Slice the lemons in quarters, leaving the end intact so they are split open into fours, but still "whole" lemons. Rub each lemon in salt (about 1 tablespoon per lemon), making sure to press salt into the flesh and cover the rinds. Place the lemons in a clean glass jar, and press down to expel some juices. Cover and store on the counter to monitor progress for three days. Over the next several days, the jar should fill, covering the lemons in their own juice. If after three days the lemons are not submerged in their juices, add some fresh squeezed lemon juice to cover fully. Store in a cool, dark cupboard for three to four weeks before using. After the lemons are completely soft and preserved, store them in the fridge and use within six months.

Cumin Black Bean Pot with Cabbage

[MAKES 6 TO 8 SERVINGS]

In fall, when the weather turns cool but vegetables are still coming in from late harvest, I love to make a big pot of black beans and invite friends over for a casual meal. The beans are good, certainly, but the stars of this dish are the fresh ingredients that make up the accoutrements. Because cabbage stores well for weeks in a vegetable crisper or root cellar, it's a great green to keep stocked in your pantry. (Use it for Peanut Soba Noodles, in this chapter.) Shredded cabbage, smoky tomatillos, and plain yogurt make an otherwise heavy dish seem light and fresh.

Olive oil
1 onion, chopped
1 tablespoon cumin seeds
2 cups dried black beans, soaked overnight and drained
2 tablespoons plus $1/4$ teaspoon salt, divided
2 cups green cabbage, sliced thin
2 tablespoons rice wine vinegar
$1/4$ teaspoon sugar
2 limes, quartered
$1/2$ cup plain yogurt

Cover the bottom of a large stockpot with a layer of olive oil and set over medium heat. When heated, cook and stir the onion until translucent. Toss in the cumin seeds and cook until the onion is soft, another 5 minutes. Add the black beans to the stockpot and cover with water by $1^1/2$ inches. Bring the mixture to a boil and stir in 2 tablespoons salt. Reduce the heat to medium-low, cover, and simmer until the beans are soft and can be mashed with the back of a spoon, about 1 to 2 hours. You are looking for a texture like thick soup, wherein some beans are beginning to break down, so add water as necessary.

Meanwhile, in a small bowl, toss together the cabbage, rice wine vinegar, remaining $1/4$ teaspoon salt, and sugar. Set the mixture aside.

When the beans are cooked, season with salt and pepper to your liking. In small bowls, set out the toppings: chopped cilantro, quartered limes, plain yogurt, tomatillo salsa (recipe below), and the cabbage "salad." Serve the beans in individual bowls and let guests garnish as they like.

TOMATILLO SALSA
4 tomatillos, halved
1 jalapeño, stemmed and seeded
1 bunch cilantro, stemmed and chopped, divided
½ teaspoon salt
¼ cup water
Squeeze of lime juice

To prepare the tomatillo salsa, place the tomatillos cut side down in a dry sauté pan over medium-high heat. Cook without disturbing until black and charred, 4 to 5 minutes. Turn the tomatillos over and cook the other sides until black and charred, for about another 4 minutes. Remove them from the pan and put in a blender, along with the jalapeño, half of the cilantro, salt, water, and a squeeze of the lime. Purée the salsa until smooth and set aside.

PANTRY NOTE: These beans will keep in your fridge for about five days. I store my beans in the fridge in the same pot I serve them in, or transfer them to a smaller bowl covered loosely with a plate. Serve any leftovers alongside corn tortillas or with a simple seared pork chop. They are great in the morning with eggs as well. Dressed cabbage will keep for four to five days in an airtight container in the fridge.

Tomato & Cinnamon Chickpeas

[MAKES 4 TO 6 SERVINGS]

This is a simple one-pot dish made complex by the layers of strong flavors in the stew—cinnamon, clove, and preserved lemon. It's the perfect choice if you're feeding a crowd, as chickpeas are not expensive. Served over a dense, plainly steamed grain, this is an uber-healthy dish that is rich and hearty. Garnish this stew with a spoonful of Herby Yogurt (in chapter 7, "Milk & Yogurt"). Plan ahead and soak the chickpeas overnight. In a pinch, canned chickpeas can be used, but they should be added after the other ingredients have stewed for an hour.

Olive oil

1 onion, sliced thin

One 28-ounce can whole peeled tomatoes

2 cups dried chickpeas, soaked in water overnight and drained

1 cinnamon stick

½ teaspoon nutmeg

1 teaspoon smoked paprika

1 teaspoon cumin, ground or smashed whole seeds

10 allspice berries

10 cloves

1 whole preserved lemon, rinsed and chopped

Cover the bottom of a large saucepan with olive oil and set over medium heat. Add onion and sauté until translucent. Add tomatoes and all other ingredients to pot. Add tomato can full of water. Set over high heat and bring to a boil, then reduce to a simmer and cook for about 1 ½ hours, until chickpeas are soft and tender. Salt to taste and serve. Garnish each individual bowl with chopped cilantro and a spoonful of Herby Yogurt.

PANTRY NOTE: This stew is great served over any leftover whole grain such as barley or quinoa. You can amend this dish by adding leftover Spiced Kibbe (in chapter 3, "Whole Grains"). It will keep for five to seven days in the fridge. Chickpeas do not freeze very well.

chapter 5

cooking with eggs

EGGS ARE ONE OF THE MOST NEGLECTED staples in the pantry. Too often I am asked "How long do eggs keep?" as they tend to sit in their cardboard cartons tucked away in the back of the fridge. Yet eggs have amazing qualities that should not be overlooked: They have a long shelf life, they are protein-rich, inexpensive, and cook up in a flash. They can be used for quick meals at home, far beyond the standard breakfast regime. Eggs can be poached, fried, baked, boiled, whipped into dressings, or used as garnish. Varying the cooking technique and incorporating eggs into lunches and dinners is a logical way to expand the role they play in the pantry. Simple boiled eggs can be left loose or cooked hard. Loose eggs are typically served at breakfast, or over a salad for a healthy lunch. Hard-boiled eggs can be stuffed or eaten simply with a drizzle of olive oil and salt. Many cultures use eggs in soup. Some Vietnamese recipes call for pickling and floating eggs in rich coconut broth, whereas a Mexican dish will call for cracking an egg into poblano-spiked tomato broth. In Italy, eggs are stirred into "ribbons" for Stracciatelli Soup (recipe follows in this chapter).

Eggs are most commonly used as necessities in cooking and baking. They are a "tool" in the kitchen. Although it's not super important to understand the exact science behind egg proteins and amino acids (and why they are critical to success in recipes), it is helpful to grasp the basics so you're able to troubleshoot if a recipe goes awry. In cakes and baked goods eggs may act as either an emulsifier (as in pound cakes) or a leavening agent (think angel food cake), and sometimes eggs play both roles.

Emulsifiers are important—they help bind liquid to oil. This is key when you're using both butter and liquids (like milk or water) in a recipe. In that scenario eggs are a stabilizer that binds together all of the fat solids so they don't separate during baking. Fats and liquids have a natural tendency to separate, and eggs stabilize and halt this process. Leavening agents are necessary as they incorporate air into batters, causing the batter to expand. When beaten eggs are used in a batter, those eggs expand in the heat of an oven, causing the batter to rise. This is how we get fluffy cakes like angel food. This is also the trick used to lighten up dense flourless batters, as in molten chocolate cakes or homemade mousses.

As a thickening agent, eggs are used in custards for freezing (ice cream) or baking (puddings). In custards and puddings, eggs and milk are cooked together to bind into a sauce (such as crème anglaise) or a custard (ice cream base). Depending on the desired outcome, custards may be cooked to a loose or firm set. (Puddings, to differentiate, often use a starch, such as cornstarch, to thicken the custard.) Custards and puddings can be made by either baking in the oven or cooking on the stovetop. Most home cooks have a tendency to think of custards as sweet recipes, but consider quiche and savory bread puddings when you're thinking of this concept.

Eggs come in varying sizes, but a good standard are those labeled "large." Choose organic eggs when possible, as the hens are not fed hormones and are antibiotic-free. From a cook's perspective, organic eggs have firmer whites and brighter-colored yolks. These raw characteristics are amplified in farm-fresh eggs.

There are environmental and social ethics involved in being an educated shopper. Vote with your dollars at the grocery store when you buy eggs. The more consumers demand organic eggs, the more producers (that is, the farmers) will need to supply. This market action of supply and demand has the ability to dictate change on a small scale. Whenever possible, support your local farm economy.

cooking with eggs
{ RECIPES }

Mom's Soft-Boiled Eggs-n-Toast
[MAKES 1 SERVING]

This recipe is so over-the-top easy that everyone should know how to make it without the aid of a recipe. Soft-boiled eggs were pretty commonplace when I was a kid. I remember ordering them at the local diner, but somewhere, somehow, they must've fallen out of fashion. I love love love soft-boiled eggs, likely because of my childhood memory of my mom making them (and me sneaking more butter into my bowl). Not quite cooked all the way, but cooked enough to smear on your toast, after you try them, soft-boiled eggs just might start making a comeback.

2 eggs per person
Unsalted butter
Salt and pepper
Toast

To make soft-boiled eggs, put the eggs in a saucepan and cover with cold water. Bring to a boil over medium-high heat. Once boiling, cook 1 minute (just 1!) for a medium-set egg (the yolk will be runny and the whites a bit loose). If you prefer a firmer white, leave for another 20 to 30 seconds, then remove immediately. Run the egg under cold water until cool enough to handle.

Using the back of a knife, crack the egg's shell. Once the shell is cracked, use a knife to slice through and cut the egg in half. Scoop out the egg using a small spoon and serve in a bowl, with a hunk of butter and a generous dose of salt and pepper. Toast is a nice partner for these eggs.

PANTRY NOTE: Try these with the Whole Grain Bread in chapter 1, "Stocking the Pantry."

Lovage & Smoked Salmon Hard-Boiled Eggs

[MAKES 1 SERVING]

This recipe is one of the fastest, most nutritious breakfasts I know of—so quickly prepared that I can eat it on the go. It's a pretty little thing and feels gourmet even though it comes together in minutes. These eggs can also be served as appetizers and are quite economical (eggs are not an expensive staple). Lovage is an easy-to-grow perennial herb (see the passage on lovage in chapter 9, "The Pantry Garden") that no garden should be without, although you can substitute fresh parsley or chervil in this recipe, both of which are just as delicious.

> 1 egg
> 1 lovage leaf
> 1 tear of smoked salmon (or any smoked fish)
> Olive oil
> Salt and pepper

To make a hard-cooked egg, put the egg in a saucepan and cover with cold water. Bring to a boil over medium-high heat. Reduce the heat to medium-low and simmer the egg for 6 minutes. Strain the water and set the egg aside to cool. (You can also plunge the egg into an ice-water bath to stop the cooking and speed up the cooling process, but this is not necessary.)

Crack open the hard-cooked egg, peel it, and cut in half lengthwise. Lay the lovage leaf on top of the yolk, top with a slice of smoked salmon, and drizzle with olive oil. Season with salt and pepper to taste.

PANTRY NOTE: Hard-boiled eggs can be kept in the fridge for one week, so it's smart to make extra.

Stracciatelli Soup

[MAKES 2 TO 3 SERVINGS]

This was a popular dish among the Italian ladies in my grandma's old neighborhood in Queens. Mrs. Collelouri, it's rumored, taught my mom and aunts how to cook Italian food. I remember long days at her house—something was always simmering in the kitchen or pasta dough was being shaped into ravioli. Stracciatelli was an easy lunch dish made with typical pantry ingredients to keep us kids happy while the grown-ups cooked all day.

Most people think of soup as cold-weather food, but this is light and delicate enough to serve even on the hottest day. My mom taught me how to make stracciatelli when I was old enough to man the stove unsupervised. It might have been the first time that I used both hands in cooking—one to pour a beaten egg into hot broth, the other to continuously stir the soup—a skill in dexterity that has served me well ever since.

> 2 to 3 cups vegetable or chicken stock
> Salt and pepper
> 1 egg
> 1 tablespoon semolina flour

Heat up the stock in a medium saucepan on medium high until small bubbles appear (a gentle boil). Season with salt and pepper to your liking. Lightly beat the egg and semolina flour in a small bowl. Slowly pour the egg–flour mixture into the stockpot, and after just a few seconds, stir the stock quickly with a fork. Cook for another minute or so at a low simmer. Serve in small bowls with a grating of fresh Parmesan, if you like.

PANTRY NOTE: Fresh tender herbs like parsley, sorrel, or chervil are nice additions to this soup. If you don't have semolina flour, it's okay to omit it.

Hand-Whipped Aioli

[MAKES ABOUT 1 CUP]

Homemade aioli is worth the effort of whipping. It takes mere minutes to make, and it tastes infi-nitely better than any store-bought brands. When I first started making aioli, I would whisk the egg and oil like a madwoman, fearing that if I didn't, I'd "break" the eggs and ruin it. Truth is, you can whisk pretty quickly (without going crazy), and that should work. Handmade aioli is especially deli-cious when you add a bunch of chopped fresh herbs for flavor. I prefer tarragon, but fresh parsley is also nice. This recipe is a great workout for your shoulders!

> 1 egg yolk
> ½ tablespoon Dijon mustard
> Dash of salt and pepper
> 1 cup light oil, such as grapeseed or canola oil
> ¼ lemon, juice only

In a medium-sized bowl, whisk together the egg yolk, Dijon mustard, salt, and pepper. While whisking continuously, drizzle in the oil at a near trickle. When you notice the mayo getting fluffy, pour in the rest of the oil in a slow, steady stream, whisking all the while. Your arm will get veeeery tired, but don't give up! When the aioli is emulsified and you have about ½ cup of it, whisk in the lemon juice. Season with salt and pepper to taste. Fold in herbs, if using.

Use immediately or refrigerate the batch.

PANTRY NOTE: I often use olive oil in my aioli. The flavor is a bit stronger, but I like it. Homemade aioli can keep in the fridge for several days and up to one week. If you have leftovers, consider adding a bit of grated lemon peel and serve as a tasty dip for chopped raw veggies.

Aioli Variations

Aioli can be used as a side or a garnish in many dishes. Using aioli is an easy way to infuse a meal with flavor. Alongside simply grilled meats, aioli lends a luxuriously smooth texture in an otherwise chewy mouthful. Aioli should not be relegated to merely a spread; it can be used as a dip for fresh vegetables as well as fried foods. Using the basic recipe provided as a base, try the following combinations to add subtle flavor to your next meal.

TO ACCOMPANY BEEF:

3 parts aioli : 1 part finely chopped roasted red
   or green pepper : splash of sherry vinegar
5 parts aioli : 1 part chopped fresh marjoram : 1 part
   chopped fresh thyme : 1 part sumac (or smoked paprika)

TO ACCOMPANY EGGS:

2 parts aioli : 1 part chopped fresh chervil or dill
2 parts aioli : 1 part ground smoked paprika

TO ACCOMPANY FISH:

2 parts aioli : 1 part chopped fresh basil : 1 part lemon juice
3 parts aioli : 1 part grated orange peel : pinch of red chile flakes

TO ACCOMPANY VEGETABLES:

2 parts aioli : 1 part chopped fresh tarragon
2 parts aioli : 1 part chopped fresh mint
2 parts aioli : 1 part grated lemon peel

Baked Eggs with Kale & Crusty Bread

[MAKES 2 TO 3 SERVINGS]

I love eggs served with a side of sautéed greens. If I can eat greens at every meal, I will, and sauté-ing chard, kale, or spinach with garlic alongside an egg is a culinary match made in heaven. This is a one-pot-only meal, perfect for a dinner when you have only eggs in the fridge for a "main" ingredient. The dish can be made with little fuss and attention. Serve a crusty piece of bread along-side, and it's a meal that can be made at a moment's notice and feed lots of mouths for cheap. The only thing needed from the grocery should be the greens, otherwise all of these ingredients are pantry staples.

2 to 3 strips bacon *(optional)*
Olive oil
Half onion, thinly sliced
2 cloves garlic, crushed
1 bunch kale, cut into ribbons, crosswise, starting
   with the stem end
Pinch of red pepper flakes
Salt
3 eggs
Toasted baguette, rubbed with raw garlic clove

Preheat the oven to 350 degrees F.

Cook the bacon in a large, deep-sided ovenproof sauté pan over medium heat, about 7 to 10 minutes or until brown. Pour off the excess fat, remove the bacon, and set aside. Coat the bottom of the same pan with olive oil. Add the onion and garlic, stirring until soft and slightly brown, about 10 minutes.

Working in batches, put the kale in the sauté pan and cook until wilted, turning continuously 5 to 7 minutes. Toss in the red pepper flakes and season with salt. Fill the sauté pan with an inch of water and cover, bringing to a simmer. Cook until the kale is tender and drain off any residual liquid.

Increase the heat to medium-high. Make three "pockets" in the kale and crack an egg in each. Leave untouched for 2 to 3 minutes, allowing the bottom of each egg to set. Cover and put the pan in the oven until the egg white is set but the yolk is still runny, about 6 to 10 minutes.

Garnish with crumbled bacon. Serve on a plate, alongside toast.

PANTRY NOTE: You can easily substitute other greens for the kale in this recipe—chard or spinach work well.

Ravioli

Using leftovers cleverly is the perfect way to keep food fresh and interesting. Sautéed greens can be incorporated into a quick homemade ravioli filling. Finely chopped and cooked kale or chard can be mixed with a few spoons of ricotta cheese, a twist on a traditional cheese filling. This works well with grilled radicchio, endive, spinach, and basil as well. Let leftovers dictate what you use.

Although soft cheese is a classic filling, there are many other options. Boil flavorful vegetables like beets, carrots, winter squash, or peas and mash them to a smooth pulp for a filling. Season with fresh herbs or some Parmesan and fill as you would normally. Ground nuts also make great fillings. Try a coarsely ground mix of pine nuts and basil for a quick homemade pesto filling. You can also use leftover meat—roasted pork or hamburger—seasoning to taste before filling.

To shape the pasta (see Hand-Rolled Pasta in chapter 1, "Stocking the Pantry"), cut each sheet of pasta into 3-inch squares. Put a small teaspoon of filling in the center and fold together opposite corners for a triangular-shaped ravioli. If the seal is not firm, dampen the edge of the pasta with your moistened fingertip—the water acts as glue. Work from the center out, as it's important to press out any air around the filling before you seal. This ensures that each ravioli will maintain its shape and not break when you boil it. Shaped ravioli can be frozen and kept in the freezer in a plastic bag.

Over Easy with Tomato & Polenta

[MAKES 4 SERVINGS]

I keep coarse cornmeal in the cupboard at all times, as it's a go-to meal when I don't have time to think about what I have to cook. Polenta is a substantial dish made from ground cornmeal, served porridge-style—thick and creamy. There are several ways to cook polenta. As with most things in the kitchen, I opt for the quickest, most efficient way and dispense with cooking polenta in a double boiler for hours.

While the polenta is cooking, I'll whip together a hearty gravy made with some sort of tomato sauce or tomato paste and leftover jus from chicken drippings (see chapter 2, "Kitchen Economy"). The gravy elevates this recipe to dinner status—a great casual meal to serve friends. A little polenta goes a long way, and you won't spend much money on ingredients. The entire dish is made up of pantry staples and leftovers.

> 3 cups water, chicken or vegetable stock, or milk
>   (or a combination of the three)
> 1 cup coarse cornmeal
> 2 tablespoons unsalted butter
> 1/4 cup freshly grated Parmesan
> 1/2 teaspoon salt
> 1/4 teaspoon freshly ground black pepper
> Olive oil
> 4 eggs
> Rich Tomato Gravy (see the recipe in chapter 2, "Kitchen Economy")

Heat the liquid in a medium saucepan over medium-high heat and bring to a boil. Add the cornmeal, a little bit at a time, whisking to incorporate. Lower the heat to medium-low and stir frequently and rigorously, cooking for about 30 minutes or until the polenta is soft and thick. Remove from the heat and add the butter, Parmesan, salt, and pepper. Cover and set aside for 5 to 10 minutes to rest.

Meanwhile, cover the bottom of a medium sauté pan with olive oil and heat over medium-high. When heated, crack in the eggs. Cook 3 to 4 minutes, until the outer edges of the whites are crispy and brown. Use a spatula to flip the eggs yolk-side down and cook for another 2 minutes, making sure to leave the yolks runny.

Serve a helping of polenta in shallow bowls. Top with one egg each and a few spoonfuls of the tomato gravy. Garnish with chopped fresh parsley, if desired.

PANTRY NOTE: This dish is excellent served with a simple sauté of garlic and greens, such as broccoli rabe or chard. You can easily increase the proportions on the polenta to make leftovers for fried polenta squares. For a hot breakfast cereal, be sure to reserve some polenta before you season with Parmesan, salt, and pepper.

Easy Bread Pudding

Bread pudding is a baked dish made quite simply with cubes of bread, milk, and eggs. These ingredients are pantry staples, so keep this inexpensive dish in your pocket for a quick weekday meal or to feed many mouths. Milk is added to the bread cubes for moisture and eggs add volume and create a custard-like texture—hence the name "pudding." Any bread item makes a great base: scraps of day-old bread, leftover stuffing, cake, cornbread, or muffins. This is a great way to use leftovers that have turned dry with age. In fact, bread puddings work best when the cubes are a bit stale and dry; the custard will soak into the crumb and leave the final dish both chewy and rich.

Add seasoning and flavors to suit the occasion. Sautéed or roasted mushrooms, onions, and fresh herbs can be used for savory bread puddings. Squash works well also: Try using roasted winter squash with sage leaves for a winter comfort dish. Just remember to season with salt and pepper! Dried fruit and homey spices like cinnamon and clove can be used for a dessert bread pudding, as can chocolate shavings and roasted nuts. Be sure to add some sweetness to a dessert bread pudding—sugar, brown sugar, or honey will work. Add what you have and what you like; this is a great dish for experimentation in the kitchen. No recipe required!

Keep these proportions in mind when making bread pudding: 1 cup cubed bread + 1 egg + ½ cup milk or cream = 2 servings. They will give you a nice balance between bread and custard. If you're after a really moist, custardy dish, add one more egg and a splash of cream. Bake covered for about 40 minutes in a 350-degree oven, removing the cover for the last 15 minutes of baking.

Pavlova

[MAKES 6 TO 8 SERVINGS]

I discovered Pavlova after I started making ice cream at home and had extra egg whites to use. Pavlova is a baked meringue dessert traditionally topped with simple fruit left unadorned. Because Pavlova is so sweet, there is no need to add sugar to the fruit on top. In addition, the acids will help to alleviate what would otherwise be an over-the-top dessert. Often I save the Pavlova and crumble it into bits so I can use it later as an ice cream or dessert topping. And more times than I care to admit, I've eaten a big hunk in the morning, floating its billowy sweetness in a pool of tangy yogurt.

> **6 egg whites**
> **³/₄ cup caster sugar, divided**
> **1 cup powdered sugar, sifted**

Preheat the oven to 300 degrees F. Trace an 8- or 9-inch circle on parchment paper and line a baking sheet. Set aside.

Beat the egg whites in a standing mixer until foamy and thick, usually about 3 to 4 minutes. Pour in half the caster sugar and beat until incorporated. Add the remaining sugar and beat until the mixture forms firm peaks. Using a fine-mesh strainer or sifter, shake powdered sugar over the meringue. Using a rubber spatula, fold in the powdered sugar, making sure to incorporate it well. (It will take several folds to incorporate well.)

Using an offset spatula (or butter knife), spread the meringue into a uniform disc on the parchment. Place the baking sheet on the center rack of the oven. Bake for 30 minutes, then reduce oven temperature to 250 degrees F. Bake for another 45 minutes, until slightly golden, and turn off the oven, leaving the meringue to dry out overnight. Do not open the oven door!

Serve the next day with the crushed fruit of your liking—passion fruit, berries, or stewed peaches (see Hibiscus Peaches in chapter 8, "Small-Batch Preserving") work well. You can also serve with a generous dusting of cocoa powder for a subtle chocolate flavor.

PANTRY NOTE: Caster sugar is a super-fine sugar that dissolves quickly in liquids (see the pantry list in chapter 1, "Stocking the Pantry"). Pavlova holds at room temp, loosely covered with parchment paper, for a week. Crumble up any leftover bits and store in a glass jar in the freezer for ice cream topping.

chapter 6

nuts

NUTS ARE THE GREAT PANTRY UNDERDOG. Often relegated to the occasional baked good or salad topping, nuts are easy to overlook when considering pantry-to-plate options. Nuts are actually seeds or fruits, wherein the nut meat is the edible heart lying within a hard protective shell. They are the ultimate hunter-gatherer food. They fall from the tree and can be easily harvested, although it may be hard to discern what a fresh-fallen nut looks like. Nuts are most commonly seen in their shelled form, and therefore it's easy to lose sight of their natural existence. Most nuts live inside another larger hull. Walnuts, for instance, are encased in a thick green pod that looks almost like a lime. The pod breaks down and falls away to reveal the hard shell that is more recognizable, but that process takes a long time. (Incidentally, that pod will stain your hands black for days.) Walnuts must be cured (sometimes for up to a year)—a process that can be sped up in a low-temperature oven.

Nut meat may be served raw, toasted, crumbled, and puréed. All manners of preparation add considerable texture to a dish. Nuts can be creamy and smooth (like almond butter). Nut butters are not just for sandwiches and toast; rather, they can be used to make rich sauces and savory dressings. Ground up to a paste, nuts act as a thickening agent. Nut meals are crumbly and dry (like pistachio meal) and can be made at home by toasting and crushing the nuts into a fine meal or "flour." Nut meals act as a sort of flour in recipes. They can be added to cakes, used in such savory recipes as stuffing, or treated like bread crumbs to crisp up and coat fried foods.

Purchase nuts raw when possible, and roast at home as called for in recipes. Whole roasted nuts have a full flavor and give a nice meaty feel to dishes. In baked goods like brownies or carrot cake, nuts add an unexpected richness. Toasted nuts often top salads for that same reason—to satiate.

Nut milks are made by steeping nuts in water and puréeing. Treat these milks as heavy cream in recipes for vegan variations of your favorite dishes. You can purchase commercial versions of nut milks, but steer clear of those with added sugar. Coconut milk (the canned variety) is a staple in Asian and Indian cooking, and is a reasonable substitute for those who are dairy intolerant or who follow a vegan diet. Coconut milk is offered in a low-fat form as well, although the regular-fat version is much more flavorful. Canned coconut milk has a shelf life of up to a year. "Cream" will collect on the surface, however, and should be stirred into the milk before measuring out for a recipe. Nut milks are a creamy alternative to chicken or vegetable stock and water when cooking soups or stews, and can be cut with stock or water using equal parts to make a velvety broth.

All nuts are high in fat and calories—not good if you plan on eating a pound of cashews every day, but excellent if you add them to your diet as a more earth-friendly alternative to meat. High in protein, nuts contain a reasonable dose of your daily vitamin and mineral needs. The fats in nuts are unsaturated (mono- and polyunsaturated, to be specific), and therefore they are lumped under the "good fat" category. These heavy oils, however, will spoil if stored too long, turning a nut rancid. The higher the fat content, or oil, the quicker the nuts will spoil. Because of this, purchase nuts in small-enough quantities that you will use up quickly. Store nuts in glass jars in cool, dark cupboards. If you have room in your freezer, store them there instead, where they will keep fresh for a much longer time. A bit on nut culture and storage . . .

ALMONDS. They are not, in fact, nuts. Rather, almonds are considered stone fruits, like peaches or apricots. Almond trees need to be pollinated to produce this fruit. When, a few years back, colony collapse disorder (the sudden disappearance of large populations of honey bees) was discovered, almond stocks were in danger and their price per pound increased. There are both sweet and bitter almonds, although the sweet varieties are used most often in cooking; the bitter almonds are reserved for oils and extracts. Almonds have a longer shelf life than some nuts and are okay stored at room temperature in a cool, dark cupboard.

CASHEWS. These grow on shrubs and sit in their shells under an edible fruit that is best eaten immediately and therefore seldom exported. Cashews are sold shelled, as the protective layer between nut and shell is a skin irritant. Heavy with fat, cashews must be used quickly or stored in the fridge, sealed in a glass jar or plastic bag.

COCONUTS. These are a tropical nut eaten fresh or dried. When choosing a fresh coconut, make sure you can hear liquid (coconut water) sloshing about inside; the nut should feel heavy. Coconuts are dense with saturated fat—the "bad" kind—and thus go rancid quickly. Keep dried coconut flakes in the fridge, well wrapped in airtight plastic. Coconut milk in cans will keep for many months in the pantry.

PECANS. Indigenous to the United States, pecans grow wild and are also cultivated. They are prevalent in Southern cooking, most popularly, no doubt, in pecan pie. Sometimes sold in their shells, they store longer in this state. If purchasing shelled pecans, use them quickly or store in the fridge in a glass jar or airtight plastic bag.

WALNUTS. Falling from beautiful tall trees in early summer and through fall, depending on the species, these nuts have been adopted by many cultures and therefore present one of the most flexible nuts for cooking. Americans use walnuts most often in baked goods, whereas many Middle

Eastern recipes call for walnuts in rich sauces and stews. Italians use them in pestos and to make liqueur. Walnut meat is pressed and sold as walnut oil—an expensive yet fantastic addition to salads. Store walnuts in the shell in a cool, dark cupboard. Once the shell is removed, eat them within a month or store in the fridge in a glass jar or plastic bag.

Walnut Sauce

Nuts have terrific versatility and can be used in many creative ways. Take walnuts, for example. I like to make a sauce of milk-soaked bread puréed with walnuts. By mastering this simple technique, I can use Walnut Sauce again and again, introducing variations that make it perfect on chicken or pasta, as a dip, and much more.

As a start, soak any leftover bread (wheat, artisan, rye) in milk until soft. Put the bread into a blender or food processor with equal parts walnuts and purée until smooth. If you prefer a chunkier sauce, don't blend for too long. If you prefer a smoother, thin sauce, even out the texture by adding more milk or some water. Once you have this base, you can add various ingredients and flavor to your liking.

Garlic can be added in small quantities or en masse if you like a raw-garlic bite. Adding spices (like the paprika-scented sauce in Walnut & Garlic Chicken, in this chapter) is an easy way to adjust the flavor. This purée is excellent served as an appetizer alongside crudité, or in place of hummus with grilled pita and sliced tomatoes. This basic recipe also acts as a sauce to pasta—the entire meal can be cooked in 15 minutes. As a variation, toast the walnuts first (bake at 350 degrees F for 10 to 15 minutes), then add freshly grated Parmesan and olive oil while processing. Prepare pasta and use a cupful of pasta water to thin out the sauce if necessary. Toss sauce with cooked pasta and serve with a handful of toasted whole walnuts for texture. Garnish with chopped fresh parsley and grated Parmesan.

Incidentally, skordalia is a variation on the same technique. A traditional Greek side or dip, skordalia can be made with milk-soaked bread and garlic, but leave out the walnuts. Serve with some fresh chopped mint alongside skewers, fried fish, or boiled beets.

nuts

{ RECIPES }

Spiced Pecans

[MAKES 1 CUP]

I owe this recipe to my good friend Rusty—a man who pulls together a mean flower arrangement and has a keen understanding of Moroccan food. He made these nuts at an import sale years ago, and I couldn't pull myself away from the buffet table to shop. I emailed him in a fit to get the recipe, and he promptly responded—from poolside in Marrakech. This is the perfect recipe to pack for a camping trip or to serve alongside a cheese platter, fancying up the boring cheese-and-cracker platters that have become a near epidemic as of late. These spiced pecans are also wonderful served crumbled over any green salad.

4 tablespoons sugar for pan, plus 2 tablespoons for bowl
1 teaspoon ground cinnamon
1 teaspoon ground cayenne
1 teaspoon ground turmeric
1 teaspoon ground paprika
1 teaspoon freshly grated nutmeg
1 teaspoon salt
¼ cup peanut oil
1 cup shelled pecans

Before you start, measure out your sugar and spices and have ready a large glass bowl. You'll need to work quickly once the nuts are toasted.

Cover the bottom of a large, deep-sided sauté pan with the peanut oil; let it pool a bit. Heat over medium-high and, when the oil is beginning to ripple slightly, toss in the pecans, stirring continuously so they don't burn. When the pecans start to smoke and brown, add 4 tablespoons of the sugar and toss, toss, toss! You don't want to burn that sugar.

After the sugar is dissolved and the nuts are well coated, use a slotted spoon and put the nuts in the glass bowl with the remaining sugar and the measured-out spices and salt. Working quickly, stir to combine. When the mixture has cooled slightly, taste and adjust the flavors, making them more salty-spicy to your liking.

Pour the spiced pecans onto a sheet pan to cool. When completely cooled, store them in a glass jar in the cupboard.

PANTRY NOTE: You can easily multiply this recipe for bigger batches. Spices can be swapped as well. If you don't have turmeric, for example, try curry powder or garam masala. These candied nuts keep nearly indefinitely but taste freshest when eaten within four to six weeks.

Toasted Almond Crackers

[MAKES 5 DOZEN CRACKERS]

These crackers are easy to make and require very few ingredients. The sweet almond flavor in this recipe goes well with all types of cheese, but I love a sharp cheddar the best. You can make home-made almond meal by grinding toasted almonds in a food processor until delicate and fine—just be sure to watch carefully, because nuts go from finely ground to nut butter in mere seconds.

> 1 cup ground almond meal
> $^3/_4$ cup whole wheat pastry flour
> $^1/_2$ cup all-purpose flour
> $^1/_3$ cup brown sugar
> $^1/_2$ teaspoon salt
> 1 stick (8 tablespoons) unsalted butter, cut into small pieces
> 2 tablespoons ice water
> 1 egg yolk, beaten

In a food processor, pulse together the almond meal, whole wheat pastry flour, all-purpose flour, brown sugar, and salt until combined. Slowly add the butter and pulse until the dough resembles coarse crumbs.

With the food processor running, add the ice water just until the dough comes together. Stop the machine immediately, turn the dough out onto a counter, and shape into a small disc. Scrape up the dough, wrap it in plastic wrap, and refrigerate it for at least 30 minutes.

Preheat the oven to 350 degrees F. Line a sheet pan with parchment paper and set aside.

Remove the dough from the refrigerator and halve. Roll each half into $\frac{1}{8}$-inch-thick sheets. Cut into small square crackers using a knife or a small cookie cutter (for more even crackers). Put the cracker dough on a parchment-lined baking sheet, leaving a bit of space between crackers but not much. (The crackers won't spread much, as a cookie would.) Roll out and cut the remaining dough, and add it to the baking sheet. Using a pastry brush, dab the tops of the crackers with a thin film of egg yolk.

Sprinkle with coarse salt and bake 12 to 15 minutes, until golden brown and crispy.

PANTRY NOTE: These crackers are best stored in parchment paper—just fold them up in the same paper you bake them on. They'll keep for ten days or so. These crackers also freeze well. Double up your batch and bake them all, freezing in an airtight plastic bag until ready to use. They will need about 30 minutes to defrost.

Spice Cupboard

There are those who measure out spices in a recipe, and those who grab a pinch and toss it in, hoping for flavor nirvana—tasting and tossing until the dish hits the "just right" mark. Being firmly of the second group, I find that my spice cupboard overflows with bags of loose spices and is a key component in my cooking. Spices and dried herbs are a foundation of recipes and therefore of a home pantry. As with much of my cooking, I pull from various cultures and try something new once every couple of months. Turkish spices include sumac, chiles, and mint. Asian food relies on ginger, sesame, and citrus. Mediterranean accents include cumin, dill, and cinnamon.

Plenty of spices are sold in two forms—whole and ground. I opt for whole spices more often than not, and grind them in my mortar and pestle when I need them. Grinding spices on demand releases oils from the seed and impacts the flavor considerably. This is particularly true of nutmeg—a great spice for tasting and comparing forms. Others are best fresh, mostly the green herbs that are so easy to grow (see chapter 9, "The Pantry Garden"). Thyme, rosemary, oregano, mint, and basil tend to lose flavor quickly when dried. Some herbs actually do well when dried—dill, marjoram, and sage.

Spices are best stored in a cool, dark place away from any heat source. I keep my spices in a drawer in my kitchen and fill small bottles with spices often. Dried spices will lose pungency and flavor over time, so it really is best to purchase them often. I lean on shopping in the bulk spice section of my grocery store. Typically, health food or natural food stores carry bulk spices. Purchase small, usable amounts and replenish your stock often. Here are my lists of must-have spices, good-to-have spices, and bonus spices:

MUST-HAVE SPICES
Black peppercorns, cayenne, cinnamon, cloves, coarse salt, cumin, curry powder, marjoram, red pepper flakes, whole coriander

GOOD-TO-HAVE SPICES
Allspice, caraway, chamomile, dill, fennel seeds, garam masala, sesame seeds, whole nutmeg

BONUS SPICES
Anise seed, cardamom, lavender, mustard seed, salt blends, star anise, sumac, turmeric, various red chile flakes in varying "heats"

Potato Gratin with Cashew Cream

[MAKES 4 SERVINGS]

My good friend Ronny is engaged to a great little lady who has slowly become my pal over the course of many dinners and drinks out on the town. Thing is, I consider Catherine a bit of a culinary challenge: she's a non-gluten-eating vegan. It's a total kitchen nightmare for a girl like me, who uses butter and chicken stock like it's going out of style. I have since made it my personal mission to cook Catherine fantastic-tasting vegan meals. I also hope to teach her a few tricks of the trade so she can make inventive food for herself at home that also leaves Ronny satisfied (being the meat lover that he is). I'm sure this formula will lead to lifelong culinary bliss!

I read about nut creams some time ago and only recently started using them with regularity. I've tried this recipe with almonds and cashews, and I've decided that cashews are the best. The key is to focus on flavor, so I've added a healthy dose of herbs and salt. This dish can be assembled one day ahead and baked on demand.

CASHEW CREAM
1½ cups boiling water
1 cup raw cashews
1 tablespoon nutritional yeast
Salt

6 Yukon, red, or purple potatoes (about 2 pounds),
    cut into about ¼-inch-thick slices
1 teaspoon salt
4 teaspoons chopped fresh thyme
4 teaspoons chopped fresh sage
Freshly ground black pepper
Nutmeg, freshly grated if possible
Bread crumbs

Prepare the cashew cream first. In a medium-sized glass bowl, pour the boiling water over the cashews and let sit for at least 15 minutes and up to 30. Stir in the nutritional yeast. Purée the mixture in a blender on the highest setting for about 3 minutes, until the consistency is smooth and creamy. Season with salt to taste. Set aside.

Preheat the oven to 375 degrees F. Now, on to the potato gratin. Bring a pot of water to boil and blanch the potato slices, about 2 minutes or until just softened. (You can also fry them up in some olive oil, if you prefer a crispier potato, which takes a bit longer.) Drain.

Cover the bottom of an 8-inch-round baking dish with a single layer of potato slices. Sprinkle with some salt, some of the chopped herbs, and a few grinds of black pepper. Add another layer and season with salt, herbs, and pepper. Continue until the baking dish is full or you run out of potatoes.

Pour in the cashew cream, almost to the rim of the baking dish. Grate nutmeg over the top, sprinkle with bread crumbs until covered, and drizzle with olive oil. Place in the oven, in the center of a sheet pan, to catch any cream that spills over. Bake for 45 minutes, or until the top is golden brown. Serve immediately.

PANTRY NOTE: This dish is best eaten day-of and will not hold well in the fridge for more than a day. Serve alongside a green salad for a perfect meal. Leftover cashew cream can be used in other gratins. For a nice variation, follow the same directions but replace the potatoes with blanched kale or mixed root vegetables. You can substitute vanilla extract for the nutritional yeast for a sweet version of cashew cream.

Carrot-Coconut Milk Soup

[MAKES 2 SERVINGS]

This recipe takes about 45 minutes from start to finish, including all of your dishwashing! It's a smooth simple soup that's big on flavor and full of vitamin A. Use bulk carrots for this—the big carrots available loose in most grocery stores. It's cheaper to buy them this way instead of the pretty bunched carrots or those little baby carrots in bags (which are, in fact, not baby carrots at all, but the same big carrots broken up and rolled to resemble a baby carrot).

This is also a fabulous recipe for carrots that have spent a little too much time in your fridge, as the final soup is forgiving and will mask any woodiness or limpness the carrots have taken on with age. Make a bigger batch so you have leftovers—I often eat this soup cold while standing in my kitchen.

2 tablespoons olive oil

1 medium shallot (about ½ cup), sliced thin

2 hearty pinches of salt

4 carrots, peeled and roughly chopped

One can (13.5-ounces) of coconut milk

1 cup water or vegetable or chicken stock

Salt and pepper

In a medium-sized saucepan, heat the olive oil over medium heat. When heated, add the shallot and one pinch of the salt, stirring until soft but not brown, about 2 minutes. Add the carrots and stir occasionally, letting them sit still and brown a bit (the shallot will start caramelizing, as well), about 8 to 10 minutes. Pour in the coconut milk and water (or stock) and reduce the heat to low. Simmer the mixture until the carrots are soft and cooked through, about 20 to 30 minutes. Remove from heat.

Carefully add the soup, in batches, to a blender. Remember to leave room in the blender as liquids expand when heated. Purée until smooth, adding a bit of water if you'd like a thinner consistency. Season with salt and pepper to taste. Garnish with a spoonful of yogurt, if desired, and serve immediately.

PANTRY NOTE: Add new flavor components to this soup by trying out different spices. A few shakes of curry, some fennel and nutmeg, or a little cinnamon and fresh ginger work very well. Leftover soup may be frozen in an airtight container and kept for four to six months. Leftovers may also be used as a "sauce" base with sautéed scallops or fish. Simply cook down and reduce the soup until thick and serve under fish that has been simply seared or grilled.

Walnut & Garlic Chicken

[MAKES 4 SERVINGS]

This quick walnut sauce is the perfect accompaniment to cold chicken. Best served room temp, it takes advantage of day-old bread and leftover roast chicken. The milk softens the bread, making the whole dish velvety and smooth. Although whole milk is fantastic (particularly if it's local and raw), I have used low-fat milk in this recipe and barely noticed the difference. You can also fudge on the amount of garlic. If you love it, add more. Don't love garlic? Add less.

> 2 thick slices artisan bread, cut into 1-inch cubes (about 2 cups)
> $^3/_4$ cup whole or low-fat milk
> 2 $^1/_2$ cups shelled walnuts
> 1 to 2 cloves garlic, whole
> 1 teaspoon paprika
> $^1/_2$ to $^3/_4$ cup chicken or vegetable stock or water
> Leftover chicken, cut into pieces
>
> PAPRIKA OIL *(optional)*
> 3 tablespoons walnut oil (or olive oil)
> 2 teaspoons ground paprika

Put the cubed bread into a medium-sized bowl and pour in the milk. Let sit until the milk is absorbed and the bread soft, about 20 minutes. Meanwhile, grind the walnuts to medium-coarse meal in a food processor. Squeeze any excess milk out of the bread with your hands and add the bread to the ground walnuts. Add the garlic and paprika into the food processor and blend as well. Pour in $^1/_2$ cup of the stock or water and blend until the mixture becomes pasty. The walnut purée should hold together but run slightly and be a bit loose. Add more stock or water if it's too thick, until the texture suits you. Serve in a large shallow bowl.

To make paprika oil, stir the walnut or olive oil with paprika. Pool into the center of the walnut purée. Garnish with chopped fresh coriander leaves, if desired, and serve alongside the leftover chicken.

PANTRY NOTE: Walnut purée will keep, covered, in the fridge for ten days. If you won't use it within that amount of time, scoop off any coriander leaves and freeze the purée only in a plastic container. Defrost and rewhip by hand before serving. It will keep frozen for four to six months.

Homemade Nut Meals & Nut Butters

Nut meals and butters add rich flavor to baked goods and offer variety to traditional recipes. Nut meals may be used in place of breadcrumbs—as breading, in stuffing, or as a garnish atop savory dishes. You can also substitute nut meal for ¼ of the wheat flour called for in a recipe, but no more, because it lacks the gluten needed to help batters rise.

Walnuts, pistachios, cashews, and pecans all make wonderful butters and meals. Try using them in place of the more traditional almonds or peanuts in your next recipe. For example, substitute walnut meal for the almond meal made in the Almond–Butter Tart recipe on the following page, or replace peanut butter with homemade cashew butter in Peanut Soba Noodles (in chapter 4, "Beans & Peas").

To make nut meal at home, use blanched whole nuts. (4 ounces of nuts will yield 1 cup of meal.) Pulse nuts in the bowl of a food processor to break them into large pieces, then process until a fine meal is formed. Nuts turn from meal to butter in a matter of seconds, so watch closely and process in short bursts. (Freezing the nuts beforehand can slow the rate at which they will turn to butter.) Due to the high fat and protein content of nut meal, it has a tendency to turn rancid quickly at room temp, so store it in the freezer.

Don't confuse nut meal with nut flour, which is not easily made at home: Nut flours are made from finely ground nut meats left over after oils have been expelled from the whole nuts. Nut flour is more dry and fine than nut meal, which contains more oil, but they can be used almost interchangeably.

Nut butters are made by processing whole nuts on high speed until they become a creamy paste. (Homemade nut butters will always be grittier than store-bought super creamy varieties.) Scrape the sides of the bowl of the processor every few seconds. Add salt, if desired, and store in an airtight container in the fridge. Nut butters may be substituted for peanut butter in recipes, though some butters may contain more oil and recipes may need some adjusting to compensate.

Almond—Butter Tart

[MAKES 1 TART]

This simple tart is one of my all-time favorite desserts to make. Absolutely seasonless, its buttery and nutty filling can be used year-round with a variety of fruits. In summer, I use cherries or apricots. In winter, a thinly sliced apple or pear tastes fantastic. You can also swap pistachio nuts for the almonds, with good result. I like the filling best for tarts, but you can also smear a layer onto some puff pastry for a quick dessert.

> 1 stick (8 tablespoons) unsalted butter, room temperature
> 1/2 cup plus 3 tablespoons sugar
> 1 egg plus 1 egg yolk
> Seeds from 1/2 fresh vanilla bean (or 1 teaspoon vanilla extract)
> 2 teaspoons all-purpose or whole wheat pastry flour
> 1 cup whole almonds, toasted, cooled, and finely ground
> 1/4 teaspoon salt
> 1 Whole Wheat Tart shell, prebaked (see chapter 1, "Stocking the Pantry")
> Approximately 1/2 cup fresh fruit of your choice
> 2 teaspoons demerara sugar

Preheat the oven to 350 degrees F.

Using a standing mixer, beat the butter and 1/2 cup of the sugar until fluffy and white, about 8 to 10 minutes. Add the whole egg, egg yolk, and vanilla bean seeds, and blend to combine well. Mix in the flour, ground almonds, and salt until just combined.

Spread the filling into the prebaked tart shell. Press in your fresh fruit of choice, sprinkle with the demerara sugar, and bake for 40 to 45 minutes, or until the tart is set and golden brown.

PANTRY NOTE: If you're not making the tart straightaway, refrigerate the almond—butter filling until you're ready to use it, up to three days. This filling holds so well in the freezer that I often make a double batch. Store it in a plastic container, laying a sheet of plastic wrap directly on the surface of the almond—butter filling, to deter freezer burn. Use within six months.

Simple Pecan Crumble & Baked Apples

[MAKES 4 SERVINGS (FILLS 4 APPLES)]

Pecan crumble is one of the easiest desserts to pull together quickly, and all of the ingredients are pantry staples. I use this crispy topping for stuffing apples in the fall. Coring out an apple and filling it with a small amount of topping is my healthy version of apple pie. With crumble, you lose the extra fat and calories from butter and sugar found in a pie and essentially eat baked fruit with little crispies. If you need a large dessert, throw some fruit in a shallow dish, double the filling in this recipe, cover the fruit with it, and bake.

> 4 tart apples, cored, bottoms left intact
> ½ cup whole wheat pastry flour
> ½ cup raw oats
> ½ cup brown sugar
> ¼ cup shelled pecans, coarsely chopped
> 1½ teaspoons ground cinnamon
> 1½ teaspoons dried chamomile flowers, crushed (optional)
> ¼ teaspoon nutmeg, freshly grated if possible
> ¼ teaspoon salt
> 6 tablespoons unsalted butter, cold

Preheat the oven to 375 degrees F. Place the cored apples in a snug baking dish and set aside.

In a medium-sized bowl, combine the whole wheat pastry flour, oats, brown sugar, pecans, cinnamon, chamomile flowers, nutmeg, salt, and butter. Using your fingertips, massage the mixture together until it forms a coarse crumb and larger clumps.

Fill each hollowed apple core with the mixture, packing the filling down until the apples are brimming with crumble. Bake for 40 to 45 minutes, on the center oven rack, until the apples are soft and easily pierced with a sharp knife. Serve warm, with a scoop of Homemade Vanilla Ice Cream (see recipe in chapter 7, "Milk & Yogurt").

PANTRY NOTE: This pecan topping stores very well in the freezer, in a plastic bag, for up to six months. You can swap out the fruit on this dessert for something more seasonal by stuffing halved peaches or apricots (and splashing with a little kirsch) in summer. This can also be used as a topping for a baked fruit crisp—just be sure to double (or more) the recipe.

chapter 7

milk & yogurt

MILK IS A PANTRY STAPLE that I am never without. Like clockwork, I pick up a carton of local milk the day before I'm about to run out. Most home cooks I know use milk for drinking, eating with cereal, serving with coffee, and mixing in smoothies. It's natural to get stuck in cooking habits. It is not often that inspiration comes from a milk carton, but milk *can* be an exciting ingredient.

Milk can be used as a rich sauce in savory baked dishes (think bread puddings or gratins). Milk paired with meat is not uncommon, although it seems an unlikely pair. My mother taught me to mix milk into meatballs, and I have since evolved the concept and use milk as a braising liquid for pork shoulder. Milk may also be used as a water or stock replacement in soups. Regardless of fat content, it lends a creamy, smooth taste and texture to both chilled and hot soups. A staple in desserts and baking, milk is a key ingredient in ice cream bases and cakes. With homemade ice cream (see the recipe for Homemade Vanilla in this chapter), you can manipulate milk to take on flavors. Cooked milk can be burned and boiled down to a thick, sweet caramel sauce (traditionally goat's milk is used for this and called *cajeta*) or added to a pan of burned sugar for traditional caramel.

Milk options have broadened over the years; there are many choices, varying percentages of fat, and unlimited companies to purchase from. Steer clear of nonfat milk if possible, however: Its watery consistency does not work well in recipes, and it has been stripped of all its natural fats to a fault. Choose at least 1 percent milkfat but, if you can, purchase whole milk for both cooking and drinking. There is not enough room here to give a well-versed schooling on the issues facing national dairy farms, but suffice it to say that milk is the one item for which I *always* go organic. Organic dairy cows are not administered with the controversial genetically engineered growth hormone rBGH. The organic dairy business is quite concentrated, but this does not guarantee a more "natural" milk product or that the milk is coming from a quaint family farm. If you have an opportunity to purchase milk from a regional dairy farm, particularly milk that has not been homogenized (which indicates it has been minimally processed), I encourage you to do so.

Beyond milk, there is a big wide world of dairy available, and I count plain yogurt as an absolute *must* in the pantry. Yogurt can be purchased in varied thicknesses, from thin pourable versions to thick and creamy Greek yogurt. I elect a thinner, pourable consistency as opposed to a thicker, scoopable texture. Thin yogurts can be strained to thicken, if needed, and also take to emulsifying into soups and batters more easily than a thick yogurt. As a matter of taste and texture, full-fat yogurt is a superior choice, although nonfat yogurt works just as well in most recipes. In my own pantry I keep nonfat yogurt and use it even if a recipe specifically calls for a full-fat version. As with milk, aim for organic and try to source locally whenever possible.

Yogurt may be used in many recipes in place of sour cream or crème fraîche. It has more of a tangy taste than the latter, but otherwise works quite well. Yogurt may also be substituted for buttermilk in some recipes. Cut the yogurt with a bit of water to thin the consistency to a thick cream. In this fashion yogurt may be used as a marinade for meat—a modified version of buttermilk-soaked chicken. Yogurt works well for both sweet and savory recipes and as a healthy substitute to fats and oils in baking. Of course, yogurt is great for breakfast; prepare a bowl with a scoop of jam or fresh fruit and a handful of raw oat flakes. Many cultures—India, Greece, and Turkey, among others—use yogurt in their daily meals. Plain yogurt is a simple unadorned garnish, topping off vegetable soups to add a healthy fat or to cool down spicy grilled meat. Used in salad dressings, yogurt replaces the oil. Use equal parts yogurt and fresh lemon juice along with chopped fresh herbs to produce a subtle creamy dressing without the extra calories. Because yogurt is cultured, it will stay fresh for a few weeks if kept consistently cool in the fridge.

Butter is another pantry staple. I typically stock my pantry with two pounds of butter at a time, as it is commonly called for in recipes. Butter can be used in equal part with olive oil for sautéing. It adds great flavor, while the olive oil drops the burn point and minimizes the chance of the butter burning. Butter is, of course, essential for baking. It may be stored at room temperature, in the fridge, or frozen for backup. Butter lasts quite a long time; spoilage is typically not an issue.

milk & yogurt
{ RECIPES }

Batidos

[MAKES 1 SERVING]

Some mornings, as I'm running out the door with keys in one hand and my cell phone in the other, I suddenly realize I haven't eaten breakfast. Not eating in the morning is a cardinal sin as far as I'm concerned, so I've learned to whip up a "meal" into one small hand-held package. Most people rely on smoothies, but I have a hard time stomaching a thick shake in the morning. Instead, I opt for a combination of milk and ice and find it to be much more pleasant. These frozen milk drinks are not uncommon in South American and Asian cultures and go by the official name batido. Berries or bananas are great for batidos, but I have expanded the idea to include some other not-so-average ingredients. Try these different combinations to shake up your morning breakfast-on-the-go, or for a quick afternoon snack.

BANANA MILK BATIDO
½ cup milk
1 banana
Spoonful of flax meal
4 ice cubes

COCONUT–DATE BATIDO
½ cup milk
4 to 6 dates, pitted and quartered
¼ cup shredded coconut
Spoonful of flax meal
4 ice cubes

FIG & FLOWER BATIDO
½ cup milk
4 dried or fresh figs, quartered
1 teaspoon dried chamomile flowers *(optional)*
½ teaspoon ground fennel seed
Spoonful of flax meal
4 ice cubes

Combine the ingredients for your chosen combination in a blender and whiz on the lowest setting for 2 minutes or so. After the ice is fairly broken up, switch to a higher speed (purée or liquefy) for 3 to 4 minutes. Letting your blender run this long ensures that you won't be stuck sucking on big ice cubes and that you'll incorporate enough air to make the drink fluffy, so it feels like a proper frozen drink. Pour into a glass or a to-go thermos and hit the ground running.

PANTRY NOTE: Adding fresh herbs or flower leaves to batidos is not only delicious but adds a new flavor for your palate. Try mint, scented geranium, or garden roses. Flax meal is used only as an addition of fiber, so feel free to omit if you prefer.

Herby Yogurt

[MAKES 4 TO 6 GARNISH SERVINGS]

Yogurt can be used in both sweet and savory recipes and has a long shelf life. This recipe takes about 2 minutes to put together and is a wonderful complement to a myriad of dishes. Try it with Spiced Kibbe (in chapter 3, "Whole Grains") or liven up grilled meat or veggies.

1 cup plain nonfat yogurt
½ teaspoon ground cumin
¼ teaspoon coarse salt
2 tablespoons chopped fresh mint

Combine the yogurt, cumin, salt, and mint in a small bowl and let sit for 10 minutes before serving.

PANTRY NOTE: This yogurt will keep in the fridge for one week, stored in an airtight container.

Minted Yogurt Soup

[MAKES 4 TO 6 SERVINGS]

A few years back I attended a farm school, spending a week in the country with a bunch of food lovers eating farm-fresh goodies and learning about where food comes from. Everyone in my class brought a new and interesting culinary story to the table, and I made many wonderful friends. Chief among them is Aliye—a Turkish bombshell who knows her way around the kitchen. She introduced me to Turkish food and taught me how to make this simple soup with one of my favorite ingredients: yogurt.

1 tablespoon unsalted butter

1 tablespoon olive oil

1 onion, finely chopped

6 cups chicken or vegetable stock

$^2/_3$ cup uncooked barley

1 cup plain yogurt (nonfat or full-fat)

1 bunch fresh mint, chopped

Salt and pepper

Heat the butter and the olive oil in a large saucepan over medium heat, until it starts to bubble slightly. Stir in the onion and cook until soft, 7 to 10 minutes. Pour in the stock and bring the mixture to a boil. Lower the heat to simmer and add the barley, cooking until it is al dente, about 45 to 60 minutes. Skim 2 cups of stock from the soup and set aside.

Put yogurt in a small bowl. Slowly add stock to yogurt, whisking constantly to temper the yogurt with the hot broth so it doesn't curdle and form clumps. When blended together, add the yogurt broth to the saucepan and stir to combine. Season with salt and pepper to taste. Serve with a generous sprinkle of chopped fresh mint in each bowl.

PANTRY NOTE: This soup will hold in the fridge for four or five days. You can also freeze any leftovers. Feel free to omit or switch out the barley with another grain—wild rice, farro, or even couscous will work. Just be sure to adjust your cooking time.

Milk-Braised Pork Shoulder with Sage

[MAKES 4 TO 6 SERVINGS]

Milk-braised pork is not something you see every day, but it's not an uncommon dish either. The milk gently curdles while cooking, which may turn some off, but it can be smoothed out later in a blender. Unless, like me, you're a true food lover and all those curds wrapped around that fatty tender meat makes you want to sing and dance in your kitchen. Braising (cooking meat in a liquid) is a method of cooking wherein you can often fudge the measurements. Nothing is precise, so use this simple recipe as a guide and embellish as you like. The one rule is to salt your pork prior to cooking. I salt it straightaway when I bring it home from the butcher, then wrap it back up and put it in the fridge until I'm ready to cook.

Olive oil
3 pounds pork shoulder, salted and "cured" overnight in the refrigerator
2 onions, chopped
4 cloves garlic, crushed
8 sage stalks, leaves picked and roughly chopped, stems reserved
Pepper
Whole milk, at least 6 cups
Salt

Preheat the oven to 300 degrees F.

Cover the bottom of a large stockpot with olive oil and set over medium-high heat. When hot, place the pork shoulder in the pot. Cook on all sides until dark golden brown. (Don't move the pork around the pot—just let each side get a nice sear.) Set the pork aside on a platter and lower the heat to medium. Add the onions, garlic, and half of the sage. Cook and stir until the alliums are soft and brown, 10 to 12 minutes.

Place the pork back in the stockpot and add the remaining sage leaves and stems as well as a few grinds of pepper. Cover the pork, about two-thirds of the way up its side, with the whole milk and bring to a boil (use more milk if need be). Cover and put the stockpot in the oven and roast until the pork is fork tender, about 3 to 4 hours. Milk will curdle around the pork and appear thick and puddinglike. Remove the pork from the sauce and set it aside on a platter to rest for 15 to 20 minutes.

Now you can either purée some of the braising liquid in a blender to smooth out the gravy or leave it as is and let people ladle some on. Season the gravy to taste with salt and pepper, and serve it alongside the sliced pork shoulder.

PANTRY NOTE: Salt the pork at least a few hours before cooking, but preferably the night before. I use about 1 tablespoon of salt per pound of pork and place it in the refrigerator. You can add rosemary in this recipe or substitute it for the sage. Leftover pulled pork can be used in a sandwich for an easy next-day lunch. Make Quick Pickle Chiles, Cucumber Quick Pickles, or a fruit infusion (in chapter 1, "Stocking the Pantry") to go along with it, add a smear of Hand-Whipped Aioli (in chapter 5, "Cooking with Eggs") or Apricot Mustard (in chapter 8, "Small-Batch Preserving") and you're golden! Leftover pork also makes an excellent ravioli filling and is wonderful served with a brown butter sage sauce.

Urban Pantry Cheeses

I am not a cheese lover. I know some people go gaga over a cheese plate full of sharp cheese, soft cheese, stinky cheese, creamy cheese, but I am not one of them. As a matter of fact, I often intentionally do *not* set out a cheese plate for nibbles before a meal because (a) I think people inadvertently fill up before the meal and (b) I find the traditional cheese plate to be a bit boring. I can just see all my cheesemaker friends rolling their eyes now, but what can I say? Cheese isn't my thing. (Nor is pizza, but don't even get me started.) Having said that, I seldom have loads of cheese in my fridge, but there is a rotating cast of staples that I keep on hand because I find them to be quite flexible in their uses. I stock cheese that can be used in more than one way. These cheeses keep for weeks in the fridge, a bonus if you haven't had time to go to the grocery. If any of these cheeses do form mold, just cut it away and eat the rest. Here are my top three picks for your pantry:

(continued)

CHEDDAR. I mostly gravitate toward dry, sharp cheddars, as the flavor will carry through a dish after you've added other ingredients. I find the mild yellow cheddars at the grocery lacking in oomph or strong flavor. Sharp cheddar or cheddar-like cheeses (such as Gloustershire or Dubliner) are widely available these days and all have a hard bite and pronounced flavor. I use cheddar stirred into creamy polenta and shave curls (using a vegetable peeler) over my eggs. This is the one cheese I love on a cheese platter, as it goes so well with dried fruit and nuts. Try it with a spoonful of Apricot Mustard (see recipe in chapter 8, "Small-Batch Preserving").

CHÈVRE. Chèvre is a soft goat cheese that is spreadable and typically mild in flavor. Anyone can make a soft goat cheese at home (given access to goat's milk, that is), but I leave it to the professionals and purchase one of those small soft logs every few weeks, whether or not I need it at the time. Chèvre is a great cheese because you can use it in so many ways. I use it along with sliced and salted cucumbers as a sandwich filling. You can bake goat cheese discs dredged in homemade bread crumbs and drizzle them with olive oil to fancy-up a green salad. Try using goat cheese as a potato substitute in gnocchi. And, yes, you certainly could set a bowl out for guests to nibble on (along with a fruit infusion, see Steeping Fruit in chapter 1, "Stocking the Pantry," for various ideas) while you're getting dinner ready in the kitchen.

PARMESAN. Growing up, we always had a block of "rat cheese" around the house. Why we called Parmesan "rat cheese" I'm not certain, but I think it was because of the perfectly triangular shape. We grated this cheese liberally over our pasta, and dinner conversation tended to consist of requests to "Pass the cheese, please." As a child, I found the flavor to be too sharp for eating straight, although my sister would grate off big slices for snacking. I have since seen many a chef shave off slices of Parmesan over salads, as a garnish over grilled asparagus, or to add fragrance to soups. Use a vegetable peeler to get long thin slices. Parmesan also makes an excellent broth on its own, so I always save my rinds. A quick soak and some time over low heat, along with some herbs, will produce an easy, flavorful broth.

Spiced Yogurt Chicken

[MAKES 4 TO 6 SERVINGS]

Marinating meat in yogurt makes a superbly tender dish and uses only everyday ingredients. The meat on this chicken will cook up tender and moist, while the skin stays crispy. Mix the marinade in the morning and let the chicken soak all day. You can bake chicken in the marinade or shake off the excess for a golden brown skin.

> One 4- to 5-pound chicken, cut up into pieces
> 4 to 5 tablespoons salt
> 1 cup plain yogurt (nonfat or full fat is fine)
> ½ cup milk
> 2 cloves garlic, smashed or finely chopped
> ¼ cup chopped fresh mint
> One 3-inch piece fresh ginger, peeled and freshly grated
> 1 teaspoon ground paprika
> ½ teaspoon ground cumin
> ½ teaspoon ground cinnamon
> ½ teaspoon ground coriander
> ½ teaspoon red chile flakes

Put the chicken in a large bowl and add the salt, tossing to combine well. Add all other ingredients and fold to combine well. Cover all the chicken pieces. Marinate, covered in plastic, in the fridge all day or overnight.

Preheat the oven to 375 degrees F. Coat a large baking dish with olive oil. Remove chicken pieces from the marinade, shaking off any extra, and place the pieces in a single layer in the baking dish. It's okay to crowd pieces and have them touching. Bake for about 1 hour, on the center rack, until the chicken is cooked through and golden. Remove and serve immediately.

PANTRY NOTE: Roast chicken leftovers can be stored, covered, in the fridge for four days. Serve this chicken alongside Barley & Sweet Potato Salad or Bulgur & Citrus Salad (both in chapter 3, "Whole Grains"). Reserve bones for Resourceful Chicken Stock (in chapter 2, "Kitchen Economy"). You can substitute buttermilk for the yogurt.

Compound Butter

Compound butters are wonderful for adding flavor and garnish to a dish. Composed of softened butter and an additional aromatic, they can be intensely flavorful and rich. Traditionally, compound butters are made and then shaped into a cylindrical round log and wrapped in parchment paper. Whole thick slices are served over the final dish, allowing the butter to melt over hot food and pool on the plate. Compound butters look pretty and punch up the flavor of a dish. The butter can also be shaped into molds or scooped with a melon baller for a nice presentation.

Compound butters can be used in sweet or savory meals. Anything that can be chopped or mashed and blended easily into softened butter can be considered. Butter smoothed with crushed blueberries is a surprising addition to morning pancakes (try the Hippie Hotcakes in chapter 3, "Whole Grains"). Baked and mashed apples, figs, or pears accomplish the same—adding an unexpected forkful to an otherwise simple meal. Citrus zest is a natural fit as well.

These butters are also used in partnership with savory meals. Chopped up bits of kalamata olive added to butter is a fancy garnish for simply baked white fish or roasted chicken. Fresh herbs liven up compound butters for fish and also work nicely with rolls or bread. Dried spices add a gentle flavor to meals—try paprika or sumac. Even apple butter can be melted over roast pork, and fig butter would pair nicely with lamb. For an over-the-top luxurious meal, try blue cheese and serve over hot grilled steak.

COMPOUND BUTTER PAIRINGS
Fruit: baked and mashed apple, crushed berries,
    mashed fresh fig
Herbs: parsley, mint, basil, dill, fennel, tarragon
Savory: olives, citrus zest, minced shallot, roasted peppers
Utter decadence: blue cheese

Chocolate Buttermilk Cake

[MAKES 1 CAKE]

An easy homemade chocolate cake should be counted among the "must haves" in any recipe lineup. This quick buttermilk cake can be used for a tea cake, a breakfast treat, or a layered birthday cake. It's a great way to incorporate buttermilk into your cooking—the slightly sour fullness makes for a perfectly moist cake. The whole wheat flour adds a bit of whole grain goodness, and a splash of cognac lends a subtle earthy flavor (although you can easily omit the cognac and use all vanilla instead).

1½ cups whole wheat pastry flour
½ cup cocoa powder
1 teaspoon baking powder
1 teaspoon baking soda
½ teaspoon salt
1 cup buttermilk
½ teaspoon cognac
½ teaspoon vanilla
½ cup butter, room temperature
1 cup sugar
2 large eggs

Preheat the oven to 350 degrees F. Butter a 9-inch cake pan and set aside. Combine all the dry ingredients (except for the sugar) in a small bowl and set aside. Stir together the buttermilk, cognac, and vanilla and set aside.

In the bowl of an electric mixer, cream the butter and sugar until well incorporated, about 5 minutes. The sugar–butter combo should be light, white, and fluffy. Add the eggs, one at a time, mixing until well incorporated, making sure to scrape the sides of the bowl.

Add half of the dry ingredients and mix until just combined. Pour in the buttermilk–cognac–vanilla mixture and blend until well combined. Add the remainder of the dry ingredients and mix until just coming together. Pour the batter into the cake pan and bake for 30 to 40 minutes, or until a toothpick comes out clean. Cool the cake on a cooling rack and dust with cocoa powder or powdered sugar before serving.

PANTRY NOTE: This cake is fantastic served with Homemade Vanilla (or buttermilk) Ice Cream (see recipe below). Wrapping the entire cake with plastic wrap extends the life of the cake several days. Store at room temperature, tightly wrapped, or freeze for up to 2 months.

Homemade Vanilla Ice Cream

[MAKES ABOUT 2 PINTS]

The first time I made ice cream, I took a spoonful to my mouth and thought, "Why haven't I done this sooner?" After, I went on an ice cream-making frenzy and followed recipes I'd find to a "T." Then I started fooling around with proportions to get a consistency and flavor more to my liking. Ice cream is often made with eggs—the protein in the egg acts as a stabilizer. In simple terms, that means the egg in the recipe acts to "glue" together the fats in the milk and the heavy cream so the ice cream does not "break."

I don't like a big fatty mouthfeel on my ice cream. I prefer a happy medium, something that feels both creamy and light at the same time. This recipe does just that, using the least amount of eggs possible. If you'd like something creamier, or an ice cream with more body, feel free to add a yolk or two. You won't mess anything up—just consider it your own personal experimentation.

> 1½ cups whole milk
> ½ cup sugar
> 1 fresh vanilla bean (or 1 teaspoon vanilla extract)
> 3 egg yolks, plus 1 whole egg
> 1½ cups heavy cream

In a medium saucepan, heat the milk, sugar, and vanilla bean over medium until hot but not boiling. Remove from the heat and let steep for 15 minutes, or until the flavor tastes right. Return the milk–sugar–vanilla mixture to medium heat and warm through.

In a glass bowl, whisk the egg yolks and whole egg until well combined. Add one ladleful of the warm milk mixture to the eggs, whisking continuously. Add another ladleful and whisk until well combined. (You are tempering the eggs slowly to a warm liquid so that you do not cook them when you add them to the saucepan.)

Pour the egg custard into the saucepan with the milk and cook over medium heat, stirring continuously, for about 8 minutes. Be mindful not to boil the milk. When it is ready, the custard should lightly coat the back of a wooden spoon. Remove the custard from the heat, and strain into a large mixing bowl. (Straining will remove any curdled egg as well as the vanilla bean.) Pour the heavy cream into the mixing bowl and stir to combine.

Lay plastic wrap directly on the surface of the custard and refrigerate until cold, at least 4 hours or overnight. Freeze in an ice cream maker, occasionally scraping the sides of the bowl, until creamy and frozen. Store ice cream in an airtight container in the freezer until ready to serve.

PANTRY NOTE: Keeping plastic wrap on the surface of your ice cream extends its life by reducing the chance of freezer burn, so keep it covered! Ice cream is a fabulous medium for infusing flavors. Check out "Flavoring Your Ice Cream" (next page) for some ice cream flavor inspiration. You can easily make buttermilk ice cream to go along with the Chocolate Buttermilk Cake (in this chapter) by substituting buttermilk for the milk in this recipe and omitting the vanilla altogether. To make an ice cream with thin chocolate flakes, place bittersweet chocolate over a double boiler until melted. Pour the melted chocolate into a large mixing bowl filled with just-churned vanilla ice cream, stirring immediately and vigorously. This will create thin ribbons of chocolate in your ice cream—officially a stracciatella!

Flavoring
Your Ice Cream

Homemade ice cream has got to be one of the easiest crowd-pleasing items to keep in your urban pantry. Because you store ice cream in the freezer, it is easy to make well in advance and enjoy when guests come over or when you need to bring something sweet to a dinner. And making ice cream is a snap! Especially if you have an ice cream maker at home. When making ice cream, the process of freezing turns the liquid (ice cream custard) into a solid (ice cream) by forming ice crystals. These ice crystals get smoothed out from churning in an ice cream maker. If you just dumped the custard into a bowl, you'd get a frozen-ice-milk version. There are plenty of ice cream makers on the market small enough for an urban kitchen. I use the machine that requires keeping a canister frozen in your freezer at all times. It does not take up much space, though, and I like being able to make a batch at a moment's notice. A simple ice cream maker can be purchased for less than forty dollars these days.

It's true that you can make ice cream *without* an ice cream maker. Freeze a shallow baking dish in advance, make ice cream custard, and cool. Once the custard is cool, pour it into the baking dish and stash it in the freezer. Once the edges start to freeze (in about 40 minutes), take the dish from the freezer and whisk vigorously with a fork to smooth it out. Continue freezing and whisking every 30 minutes until frozen through. Essentially, you are acting as a human ice cream maker by breaking up the large ice crystals. The entire freezing process will take about 3 hours.

The great thing about ice cream is that it's made with dairy. And dairy of most any kind (milk, heavy cream, soy milk, coconut milk) takes very well to infusions. To infuse, heat up the milk or heavy cream and steep an aromatic in the warmed liquid, much like you would a pot of tea. Want Earl Grey ice cream? Heat up milk, add tea bags and let it steep until you like the flavor, then remove the tea bags and freeze. Super simple. You can do this with any flavor of tea, edible flower, or herb. You can even infuse milk with popcorn—yes, really! Think big and go crazy. Not only will you come up with something interesting, you'll soon find yourself considering what else you can add for flavor. And for the record, the concept of infusing milk can also be applied to other custards. Think crème brûlée, pudding, panna cotta—all those foods contain milk, which takes kindly to perfuming.

Here are some suggestions for flavor additions:

CHAI TEA. Use a tea bag or loose tea that you then strain.

CLOVE. A little goes a long way. This is a great winter ice cream.

LAVENDER. It's a very strong flavor, so be sure to check often and strain it early.

MINT LEAVES. I like to use a lot of these because I prefer a strong flavor.

PINE OR CEDAR NEEDLES. Use the tender new growth in spring and serve alongside a nut tart.

ROSE PETALS. Make sure to choose scented garden roses, not commercial roses from a florist. Rose petals are edible.

SAGE LEAVES OR STALKS. Serve with blueberry or huckleberry sauce.

TOASTED ALMONDS. Toast in the oven and chop, add to milk, then strain when the flavor is right. You can reserve the nuts for an ice cream topping or for making brittle.

TOASTED RICE. Okay, this one sounds weird, but I had this toasted rice gelato once that rocked my world. Toast white or jasmine rice in a dry skillet until fragrant. Add to warmed milk and steep. Strain. Freeze. Delicious!

chapter 8

small-batch preserving

MY MOTHER TRIED HER HAND AT CANNING when I was a kid. I remember, vaguely, the jars of graying peaches and the pucker we experienced from drinking her unsweetened Concord grape juice. Seeing and tasting the contents of those jars made me think, for a very long time, that canning was the worst possible treatment for produce. It wasn't until I was older that I became interested in preserving to stock the pantry. It started when I found a neglected greengage plum tree in a deserted backyard. A friend and I were quick and stealthy about getting those plums, nervous we'd be caught. She shook the tree with all of her weight, I ran around gathering the ripe plums that fell to the ground. Walking away with more than five pounds of fruit, I wasn't sure what to do with it all. I couldn't eat it fast enough, so I decided to do some preserving. I did some research, eventually settling on a batch of chamomile-infused jam. Preserving started as a hobby, turned into an obsession, and now is a way of life for me.

Food preservation has been around for centuries. Food may be salted, fermented, jarred up, covered in oil, dehydrated, cellared, and frozen—all as means for preservation. There was a time, of course, that preserving food was a life-or-death matter. People had to rely on their own resources and planning to survive the winter, so food preservation was vital. Now, with a focus on eating locally and seasonally, we can use the same techniques to aid in eating local all year long. Preserving and canning are perfect ways to extend the season and keep the larder stocked with fantastic farm-fresh food even in winter, when there isn't much in the ground to harvest.

The decision about what to preserve should be influenced by what produce is in season and abundant locally—either in your garden or at the farmers market. Buying food in bulk at the height of the season is a thrifty affair. It is simply a matter of supply and demand. Shoppers would be wise to take advantage of boxes of tomatoes and peach harvests from local orchards each summer. In selecting what to preserve, choose food that you have actual interest in eating throughout the year. I don't want to pickle everything I see, nor do I want to eat forty-seven jars of jam in a calendar year. This chapter includes a range of canning recipes. Using family recipes and instruction offered by both the USDA and various university extension programs, I have developed these recipes based on flavor and flexibility for using them later in meals.

Preserving does not need to be an intimidating process. There are two ways to create a safe seal on your preserving jars, either by water-bath canning or by using a pressure canner. Water-bath canning is recommended for high-acid foods like most fruits and any food that is pickled in vinegar (wherein the vinegar helps to lower the pH). Bacteria that can cause spoilage in foods is killed at 212 degrees F (100 degrees Celsius), the boiling point for water-bath canning. The low pH of fruits or vinegar inhibits an environment conducive to botulism. Water-bath canning is the method I use the most. Time spent in the water bath varies according to the food being processed, so it is important to follow directions closely and work only from tested recipes. You can easily water-bath can fruits, some tomatoes, pickles, and jams. I stick to water-bath canning, as it's the easiest to do at home in a small urban kitchen. I use a stockpot lined with a dish towel for my canning pot, and put food up in small batches. If you have a gas range, you can use a proper canning pot, which will heat up quickly. For bigger projects, the larger canning pot is a must. The alternative way to preserve food in jars is by using a pressure canner. Pressure canners allow safe preservation of most low-acid vegetables (like beans or corn) and meats because they can be heated to much higher temperatures (240 degrees F) than boiling water. This high heat kills all bacteria, including botulism. For the urban kitchen I am including only water-bath recipes here. I wish I had room for a pressure canner in my small kitchen, but I don't.

Although you should be concerned about spoilage and bacteria, if you follow recipes you should not have a problem. If a preserved good ever has a loose seal, gives off any odor, or discolors profusely, err on the side of caution and dispose of it without eating.

There are several concepts to grasp in home-canning that will alleviate the stress for a beginner:

- High-acid foods like fruits and those that are preserved in vinegar (with a pH of 5 percent) do not run the risk of botulism. Acids prevent harmful bacteria from growing. Adjust the pH in low-acid foods to prevent this bacterial growth or can at extremely high temperatures by using a pressure canner.

- Acid lowers the pH of foods and can be added by using lemon juice, vinegar, or citric acid. The pH refers directly to the acidity of foods. High-acid foods have a low pH (good for canning!), whereas low-acid foods have a high pH (needs adjusting for canning!).

- Sugar is used in canning to aid in the "set" of the fruit; essentially this means that sugar helps jam to gel. Sugar also helps to prevent discoloration and adds flavor. Sugar does not affect the "safety" of a jam.

- Pectin is naturally occurring in fruits but particularly high in the skin, membranes, and seeds (especially of apples and lemons). Pectin aids in the "set" of the fruit, much like sugar.

- Glass jars and lids do not need to be sterilized before use if your foodstuffs will be processed more than 10 minutes in a boiling water bath.
- If you live at a high altitude, don't forget that you'll need to add to the processing times given here: process jars in a water bath for an additional 5 minutes if you're more than 1,000 feet above sea level or for an additional 10 minutes if you're above 6,000 feet.
- Hot-packing refers to slightly or fully cooking fruits or vegetables before canning them. This helps remove air from the plant's cells. Raw-packing is placing a raw ingredient in a jar and then covering it with liquid (hot or cold) before canning. When fruit is raw-packed, it will often float in the liquid after sealing, which is not unsafe so much as unsightly.

And here is one personal pantry rule that I always adhere to in my kitchen: Never never never open a can of preserves when the fruit or vegetable is still in season and available fresh! Why go through the trouble of picking out the freshest, most seasonal produce, slaving over a stove to prep them for canning, time the hot water bath, and seal the jars with scientific precision, just to open the jars and eat the goodies within a week? If you're dying for some jam or pickles to eat immediately after you make them, don't go through the trouble of preserving and being mindful of pH. Just make a batch and store it in your fridge, where it will last for weeks.

Water-Bath Canning 101

This is a step-by-step guide to water-bath canning at home. There are a few options to choose from, but all work well. Be sure to set up your jars and workspace beforehand so you can establish a rhythm. Also, be mindful of the processing times given in each recipe.

CLEANING JARS. Wash your jars and lids in hot soapy water and set them to dry completely on a rack or on a clean dish towel.

PREPARING JARS. Glass jars and lids do not need to be sterilized before use if your foodstuffs will be processed more than 10 minutes in a boiling water bath or pressure canner. If jar-processing time is 10 minutes or less, jars must be sterilized before filling. Do this by placing jars in a canning pot, filling with water, and bringing water to simmer. Hold jars in water until ready to use. Alternatively, I always hold just-washed jars in a 225-degree oven until ready to use. This is not recommended by the USDA, but I'm still alive to give you the option.

FILLING THE JARS. All canned goods will need headspace to allow for expansion of the food and to create a vacuum in cooling jars. As a general rule, leave ¼ inch of head-space on all jams and jellies and ½ inch of headspace on all whole fruits. When using whole fruits, release air bubbles in just-filled jars by tapping the jar on the counter or by inserting a wooden chopstick or skewer into the jar and gently stirring the fruit. When placing lids and rings on canning jars, do not overtighten the rings. Secure just until rings have tension and feel snug. Overtightening will not allow air to vent from the jars—a crucial step in canning.

HEATING THE CANNING POT. Fill your canning pot or a deep stockpot half full of water and heat to a low boil. Hold the liquid on a very low boil until ready to use.

FILLING THE CANNING POT. If using a canning pot, place prepared jars of food on the rack in the canner. Do not stack, as you need to allow for circulation of water for proper sealing. Lower jars into the canning pot, and add enough water to cover the jar tops by an inch or more. Cover the pot and return to a boil. *Processing times begin once the canning-pot water is brought back up to a boil.* This can take as long as 15 minutes, so be sure to keep an eye on your pot and a timer nearby. You may also use a deep stockpot (best only in small-batch preserving) by lining the bottom of the pot with a dish towel and placing jars on top. This helps keep jars from clanging around on the bottom of the pot or tumbling over onto their sides. This form of canning is not universally recommended or endorsed by the USDA. I have seen plenty of farmers and European country folk use this old-school technique, and I've adapted their laissez-faire ways.

REMOVING SEALED JARS. Using a jar lifter, or a set of kitchen tongs, remove jars from the canner when the processing time has elapsed. (Remember, processing times begin once the canning-pot water is brought back up to a boil.) Set jars aside on a folded towel to cool. Make sure you *do not press* on the tops and create an artificial seal.

KNOWING WHEN JARS ARE SEALED. You'll hear the sound of can tops popping shortly—a sign that a secure seal has been made. Once the jars are cool, check the seal by removing the outer ring and lifting the jar by holding only the lid. If it stays intact, you have successfully canned your food. If the seal is loose or broken, you may reprocess in the water bath within twenty-four hours. (Be sure to replace the lid and check the jar rim for cracks or nicks and replace if necessary.) Alternatively, you can refrigerate the jar immediately and use within three weeks.

LABELING AND STORAGE. Once cool, label all jars with date and contents. Success-fully sealed jars should be stored in a cool dark place, such as a cupboard. Officially, canned goods keep for up to a year, but I have let them go a bit longer with little effect. Remove rings from jars so that they stack more easily in your cupboard.

small-batch preserving

{ RECIPES }

Rhubarb Jam

[MAKES ABOUT 5 PINTS]

Rhubarb is actually a vegetable, not a fruit as we've come to consider it. It is among the first produce available in spring, making it a great choice for kicking off the canning season. Rhubarb is
quite tart, so I add more sugar than I normally would during preserving. I choose long thin stalks
that have equal parts red and green. I do not peel the rhubarb, as I don't mind whole pieces intact in
the jam. This pretty pink jam is a total winner. For specific details on canning, follow the directions
outlined in the "Water-Bath Canning 101" sidebar.

> 4 pounds rhubarb, washed and cut into small chunks
> 4 cups sugar
> 1½ cups water
> 1 lemon, halved and juiced, seeds held in a muslin bag
>   or pouch of cheesecloth (halves reserved)

Prepare jars for canning (you'll need to sterilize jars for this recipe). Place a small plate in the freezer
(you will use this later to check the jam set). Put the rhubarb, sugar, water, lemon juice, seed bag, and
lemon halves in a large bowl and let them macerate at room temp for 1 hour. Pour the mixture into a
large pot and bring to a boil over medium-high heat. Make sure your lemon seed bag sits in the liquid
as well. (Rhubarb is a low-pectin vegetable and will benefit from the extra pectin in the seeds.) Stir
the jam constantly for about 15 minutes, then drop the heat to medium. Hold the jam at a constant
simmer, but make sure not to burn the bottom of the pot. Skim the foam from the surface as it cooks.
After 15 minutes, check to see if your jam has set. (Add a small spoonful of jam to the plate in the
freezer. Jam should hold its shape when cool.) If too loose, continue cooking over medium-low heat
until set. Remove seed bag and lemon halves and compost them.

Put the jam into sterilized jars and gently tap the bottom of the jar on the counter to release any air bubbles. Fill to the bottom-most ring, leaving headspace. Using a damp clean towel, wipe the rims of the jars and secure the lids and rings. Process in a water bath for 5 minutes if using pint jars, 10 minutes if using quart jars.

Remove the jars with tongs and let cool on the counter. When the jam is cool, remove the metal rings, check for proper seals, and label with the date and contents. Store in a cool, dark cupboard until ready to use, for up to a year.

PANTRY NOTE: Rhubarb jam is delicious served alongside roast pork, replacing the more typical applesauce. It's even better if you serve that pork with some caramelized onions! You can also substitute Scented Sugars (in this chapter) for the sugar in this recipe—vanilla or rose geranium work beautifully.

Nigella Plum Jam

[MAKES ABOUT 8 HALF PINTS]

If you can get your hands on greengage plums for this recipe, you'll be pleased you did. Greengage plums are thin-skinned and less mealy than purple plums can be. They also retain their soft green color after preserving. If purple plums are your only option, shoot for the oblong Italian plums. Nigella seeds (see the section on nigella in chapter 9, "The Pantry Garden") are ready to be harvested just as plum season begins. Infusing the jam water with this spice gives it a bit of a peppery bite, making this spread delicious with savory dishes as well as sweet. For specific details on canning, follow the directions outlined in the "Water-Bath Canning 101" sidebar.

4 pounds plums, pitted and halved

2 ½ cups sugar

1 ½ cups water

¼ cup nigella seeds, lightly crushed

1 lemon, outer peel grated, halved and juiced,
  (seeds reserved in a muslin bag)

Prepare jars for canning. You'll need to sterilize jars for this recipe.

Put a small plate in the freezer (you will use this later to check the jam set). Put the plums, sugar, water, nigella seeds, seed bag, lemon juice, and lemon halves into a large saucepan and bring to a boil over medium-high heat. Stir the mixture constantly for about 15 minutes, then drop the heat to medium-low, holding the jam at a constant simmer but making sure not to burn it.

After about 10 minutes, remove half of the plums with a slotted spoon and set aside in a small bowl. This helps keep some plums whole in the final jam. Continue cooking the rest until thickened. When the jam is thick, return the reserved whole plums to the stockpot and cook a few minutes more.

Test the jam set, using the plate in the freezer. Continue cooking on low for a thicker jam. When set is reached, remove the seed bag and lemon halves and compost them. Put the plum jam into sterilized jars and gently tap the bottom of the jars on the counter to release any air bubbles. Using a clean damp towel, wipe the rims of the jars and place lids and rings on jars. Process in a water bath for 5 minutes if using pint jars, 10 minutes if using quart jars.

Remove the jars with tongs and let cool on the counter. When the jam is cool, remove the metal rings, check for proper seals, and label with date and contents. Store in a cool, dark cupboard until ready to use, for up to a year.

PANTRY NOTE: Nigella Plum Jam is really delicious served alongside a gamy meat like roasted duck or venison chops. It also imparts a simple sweetness to a cheese-filled crepe or blintz. Fennel seeds are a great substitute for nigella seeds. You can also substitute chamomile flowers for nigella seeds in the same measurement for a more floral-scented jam. If you prefer a completely smooth jam, place nigella seeds in the lemon seed bag and leave out of the final jam.

Brandy-Spiked Cherries

[MAKES ABOUT 5 PINTS]

Nothing beats a homemade brandied cherry for the ultimate Manhattan garnish. My love of an icy Manhattan inspired me to make these cherries. Brandied cherries are a wonderful gift, so be sure to make enough for giving away as well as stocking the pantry. I seek out fancy-shaped jars for these, which make them that much more special. Choose a brandy that you actually wouldn't mind sipping. I've gone the really cheap route, and although the final product was okay, I prefer a smooth brandy to one with a sharp bite. For specific details on canning, follow the directions outlined in the "Water-Bath Canning 101" sidebar.

> 1 1/2 cups sugar
> 2 cups water
> 2 1/2 cups brandy
> 5 pounds Bing cherries, pitted (pits reserved)

Prepare jars for canning. Put the sugar and water in a large saucepot and bring to a boil over high heat. Remove from the heat and add the brandy and Bing cherries, letting the mixture sit for 10 minutes.

Pack the jars, adding only cherries until they reach the first ring on the top of the jar. Add a spoonful of reserved pits to each jar. On a folded-over dish towel (for padding), strongly tap the bottom of the jar on the counter, to help pack down the cherries. Fill the jar again, leaving 1/2 inch of headspace.

When the jars are full, bring the cherry juice back up to a boil and reduce slightly, about 15 minutes. Using a ladle or a liquid measuring cup for ease, pour hot juice over the jarred cherries, leaving 1/2 inch of headspace. Gently stir the cherries to release any air bubbles. Wipe the rims of the jars, using a damp clean towel, and place the lids and rings on the jars. Process in a water bath for 20 minutes.

While the jars of cherries are in the water bath, reduce any remaining brandy liquid over high heat until thick, like syrup. Pour this into small (4-ounce) canning jars and add a spoonful of pits to each jar. Process this syrup in a water bath, as you did for the cherries.

Remove the jars with tongs and let cool on the counter. When the jars are cool, remove the metal rings, check for proper seals, and label with date and contents. Store in a cool, dark cupboard until ready to use, for up to a year.

PANTRY NOTE: Brandied cherries can also be made and held in a large jar in the fridge, leaving them to cure for six weeks before serving. I preserve them in sealed jars so I have room in the fridge, but if you have an extra cooler in the house, by all means, spare yourself the hassle of sealing the jars. Use the leftover syrup in desserts or fancy cocktails.

Simple Sour Cherries

[MAKES ABOUT 5 PINTS]

I love love love pie cherries. They make the most exquisite tarts, jams, and more. They are not widely available, but it's worth it to ask your local orchardist if he or she grows them or knows of anyone who does. Sour pie cherries are worth the extra couple of dollars a pound you'll pay over the cost of sweet cherries. While a sweet cherry is perfect for eating fresh or soaking in brandy, sour pie cherries can't be beat for all other desserts.

I prefer to keep sugar use to a minimum. I like these cherries sweet but not too sweet. If you prefer a sugar-sweet cherry, add more sugar to your syrup. I raw-pack these cherries—I want them to be as whole and firm as possible when I open the jar. They float in the syrup unless you pack the jar densely by removing as much air as you can before and after filling the jar with syrup. For specific details on canning, follow the directions outlined in the "Water-Bath Canning 101" sidebar.

5 pounds sour pie cherries, such as Montmorency,
stemmed and pitted (reserve your pits!)

SYRUP
6 ½ cups water
1 cup sugar

Prepare jars for canning. In a large saucepan, bring the water and sugar to a boil over high heat. Reduce the heat to medium-low and keep at a low simmer until you are ready to use the syrup.

Pack the jars, adding the cherries until they reach the bottom-most ring on the top of the jar. On a folded-over dish towel (for padding), strongly tap the bottom of the jar on the counter to help pack down the cherries. They'll compress at least $1/2$ inch. Fill the jar again to the bottom ring and tap down again, compressing the cherries as much as possible without squeezing them down. Add a spoonful of cherry pits to the jar for flavor.

Once the jars are full (with $1/2$ inch of headspace), distribute any cherry juice that has accumulated at the bottom of the cherry bowl evenly among the jars. Using a ladle or a liquid measuring cup for ease, pour the hot syrup over the cherries, leaving $1/2$ inch of headspace. Gently tap the bottom of the jar on the counter to release any air bubbles. Wipe the rims of the jars, using a damp clean towel, and place the lids and rings on the jars. Process in a water bath for 25 minutes.

Remove the jars with tongs and let cool on the counter. When cooled, remove the metal rings, check for proper seals, and label with date and contents. Store in a cool, dark cupboard until ready to use, for up to a year.

PANTRY NOTE: You'll likely have extra simple syrup left after your cherries are packed. Store this in a jar in the fridge for your next canning adventure. You'll need 2 pints of sour cherries to fill a pie. I often add 1 pint plus another fruit when making a tart or pie, to extend the life of the cherries. Once open, these cherries will keep in the fridge for several weeks.

Boozy Blood Orange Marmalade

[MAKES ABOUT 5 HALF PINTS]

I'm not sure how I got the idea to add booze to marmalade, but the experiment ended up being a success. A splash of bourbon intensifies the flavor and also helps mellow out the sour edge a marmalade can have. The secret to a good marmalade is in your preparation. This is a lengthy process, so I typically make one big batch a year and then call it done. All that outer peel slicing is time consuming, so plan for a couple of hours, at least. Making this marmalade in stages helps to break it down. If you can't source blood oranges, use lemons instead, which are in season at the same time.

> 2 pounds blood oranges, scrubbed, peeled, halved, and juiced
> (seeds reserved in a muslin bag)
> 1 lemon, scrubbed, peeled, halved, and juiced (seeds reserved
> in a muslin bag)
> 3 cups water
> 2 to 3 cups sugar
> 3 to 4 tablespoons bourbon

With a vegetable peeler, remove the outer peel from both the oranges and the lemon, avoiding the white pith. Cut the peel into very thin strips and toss into a large pot. (Wider pots are better for jam-making than deep pots.)

Pour the orange juice and lemon juice into the large saucepot, along with the muslin bag of reserved seeds. Add the peels, the lemon halves, and 4 of the orange halves. Add the water and set over medium-high heat. Bring the mixture to a boil and then reduce the heat to a simmer, cooking until the rinds are soft, about 30 minutes. Cover the saucepot and put in the refrigerator for at least 6 hours or overnight.

Measure the marmalade. For every cup of citrus and liquid, add $^3/_4$ cup of sugar to the saucepot. (So, 4 cups of citrus equals 3 cups of sugar.) For every cup of citrus, measure out 1 tablespoon of bourbon and set aside. Return the saucepot to medium-low heat and cook down the mixture. Skim off any foam that forms and stir the marmalade often. After 30 minutes, add the bourbon. Put a plate into the freezer for testing the set. Cook until the marmalade gels, about 30 minutes to an hour (depending on how wide your saucepot is).

Prepare jars for canning. To test the marmalade, remove the plate from the freezer, spoon a small amount onto the cold plate, and let it sit a moment. Push the marmalade with your fingertip. If a wrinkle forms in the jelly, the marmalade is done. If it is loose and runny, keep cooking and stirring until thickened. When your desired consistency is reached, remove the muslin bag of seeds and the citrus halves, squeezing any excess juice into the saucepot. You can compost your solids.

Add the marmalade to the jars, leaving $\frac{1}{4}$ inch of headspace. Using a damp clean towel, wipe the rims of the jars, and place lids and rings on the jars. Process in a water bath for 10 minutes.

Remove the jars with tongs and let them cool on the counter. When cooled, remove the metal rings, check for proper seals, and label with date and contents. Store in a cool, dark cupboard until ready to use, for up to a year.

PANTRY NOTE: This marmalade is a consummate pantry staple because of its ability to be served with sweet or savory foods. Use this on your toast, or smear a layer on the bottom of an Almond−Butter Tart (in chapter 6, "Nuts"). You can also add some fresh garlic and water to the marmalade for a wonderful marinade and glaze for fish, chicken, or duck. Spread some on the meat and cook according to directions. I also serve marmalade on cheese plates alongside a soft creamy cheese. Store in the fridge after opening.

Indian Pickled Carrots

[MAKES ABOUT 3 PINTS OR 6 HALF PINTS]

I use tiny baby carrots for this pickle, as they are super sweet and precious. Ask at the local farmers market if they have "seconds"—produce not up to par for regular sale. Seconds are typically much cheaper, and you won't notice little nicks and bruises in a pickle. If you can't find baby carrots, cut regular-sized carrots into uniform matchsticks. These spices are very typical in Indian cuisine and add an interesting scent and flavor. Feel free to add or omit any of them, although together they work in harmony. For specific details on canning, follow the directions outlined in the "Water-Bath Canning 101" sidebar.

2 cups apple cider vinegar

³/₄ cup sugar

3 peels of lemon rind (left whole, not grated)

1 cinnamon stick, broken into 3 or 6 pieces (1 piece for each jar)

¹/₄ cup vegetable or grapeseed oil

¹/₂ teaspoon fenugreek seed

¹/₂ teaspoon black mustard seed

¹/₂ teaspoon fennel seed

¹/₂ teaspoon chile flakes

¹/₂ teaspoon coriander seed

¹/₄ teaspoon cumin seed

1-inch-long piece of fresh ginger, peeled and finely diced
    (about 1 tablespoon)

1 clove garlic, roughly chopped

¹/₂ teaspoon salt

¹/₄ onion, thinly sliced

1 pound baby carrots, peeled (or 1 pound bulk carrots,
    cut into uniform matchsticks)

Prepare jars for canning. In a medium-sized saucepot, bring the apple cider vinegar, sugar, lemon peel, and cinnamon stick to a gentle boil and hold over low heat.

In another sauté pan, heat the vegetable oil over medium-high until hot. Stir in the fenugreek seed, black mustard seed, fennel seed, chile flakes, coriander seed, and cumin seed. When the spices begin to pop (about 4 minutes), add the ginger, garlic, salt, and onion, cooking and stirring until soft and slightly caramelized, about 6 to 8 minutes. Set aside.

Pack the canning jars with the carrots, leaving $\frac{1}{2}$ inch of headspace. Pour equal spoonfuls of the spice mixture into each jar. Pour the hot vinegar liquid over the carrots, submerging them and leaving about $\frac{1}{2}$ inch of headspace. (The contents should sit just below the bottom ring on the glass jar.)

Process the jars in a water bath for 15 minutes. Make sure the seals are secure, and store in a cool, dark cupboard for at least three weeks before eating.

PANTRY NOTE: These carrots go well with grilled lamb in any form, or even as a side to a lamb burger. Serve them as a side to Apricot–Chickpea Salad (in chapter 4, "Beans & Peas") or alongside Spiced Kibbe (in chapter 3, "Whole Grains").

Apricot Mustard

[MAKES ABOUT 5 HALF PINTS]

I like diversity in my pantry. Sticking to the same recipe year after year gets a bit exhausting, and I grow tired of canning with the same recipes each season. In my quest to try something new, I decided to try a fruit mustard. Fruit mustards are not uncommon. Italians cook up fruit and add mustard to the syrup, calling it mostarda—a spicy fruity combination served alongside meat. For this recipe I make a pot of apricot jam, soak mustard seeds in apple cider vinegar, and cook them together into a thick condiment. It is similar to honey mustard, but the apricot is more pronounced and the mustard is more spicy than sweet. For specific details on canning, follow the directions outlined in the "Water-Bath Canning 101" sidebar.

> 2 pounds apricots, pitted and halved
> 2 ¼ cups sugar
> ½ cup water
> 1 lemon, outer peel grated, halved, and juiced
>   (seeds reserved in a muslin bag)
> ¼ cup brown mustard seeds
> ¼ cup yellow mustard seeds
> 1 tablespoon ground yellow mustard
> 1 cup apple cider vinegar

In a large saucepan, combine the apricots, sugar, water, lemon juice, lemon halves, seed bag, and grated peel. Over medium heat, bring the mixture to a simmer. Skim any foam from the surface as it cooks. Cook until the fruit is soft and the sugar is dissolved, about 20 minutes. Remove from the heat and, leaving the mixture in the saucepan, cover and hold in the refrigerator for at least 6 hours or overnight.

While the apricots are cooking, smash the brown and yellow mustard seeds with a mortar and pestle. Work in small batches until most of the seeds are broken and slightly ground. You can also use a spice grinder, but be sure to grind them only to a coarse meal. Put the smashed seeds and ground mustard in a small glass bowl, pour in the apple cider vinegar, and set aside, covered, on the countertop, at least 6 hours or overnight.

Prepare jars for canning. You'll need to sterilize the empty jars for this recipe.

Put a small plate in the freezer. (You will use this later to check the set.) Return the saucepan of fruit to medium heat on the stovetop and cook down until thickened and amber in color, about 30 minutes. Stir in the vinegar–mustard seed mixture. Scoop out about a cup of the apricot mustard and purée in a blender, on high speed, until creamy and smooth, about 5 minutes. Add the puréed fruit back to the pot and cook until thick and the mustard is set, about another 15 to 30 minutes. Skim foam as necessary. Remove the lemon halves and seeds from the stockpot, pressing out any mustard or remaining juice and pulp, and compost.

To test the set, remove the plate from the freezer and spoon a small amount of mustard on it. Push the mustard with your fingertip. It should wrinkle, indicating it has set. If the mustard is loose, return the mixture to the heat and cook for another 10 minutes, checking the set until the desired consistency is reached.

Add the mustard to the prepared jars, and gently tap the bottom of the jars on the counter to release any air bubbles. Using a clean damp towel, wipe the rims of the jars and put the lids and rings on the jars. Process in a water bath for 5 minutes (whether using half-pint or pint jars).

Remove the jars with tongs and let cool on the counter. When the mustard is cool, remove the metal rings, check for proper seals, and label with date and contents. Store in a cool, dark cupboard until ready to use, for up to one year.

PANTRY NOTE: Apricot Mustard is a well-matched condiment for cured meats and cheese. Make a platter for a little snack or predinner nibble for guests. It is excellent when cut with mascarpone and used as a spread. This mustard can also be used as a glaze on roasted meats. Brush mustard on the meat in the last 10 minutes of cooking. Once opened, store in the fridge, where it will keep for many months.

Ajvar

[MAKES ABOUT 4 HALF PINTS]

My grandfather immigrated from Krk, an island in Northern Croatia. As a kid, I have strong memories of him standing over a pot on the stove stirring wine into octopus or softening onions. The house always smelled of something savory and foreign. A few years back, I visited my family in Croatia, and my trip happened to coincide with the fall harvest. I spent a day picking grapes with my Slovenian cousins and an afternoon making ajvar with a neighbor. Ajvar is a smoky red pepper relish made with charred peppers and eggplant. It's a way to preserve the glut of peppers at the end of fall and can be used as a relish for meat, a sauce on pasta, or a spread on sandwiches or over eggs. For specific details on canning, follow the directions outlined in the "Water-Bath Canning 101" sidebar.

1½ pounds eggplant, cut in half lengthwise
2½ pounds peppers, red or mixed
Olive oil
1 large onion, finely chopped
1 tablespoon salt
2 tablespoons sugar
¾ cup apple cider vinegar

Preheat the oven to 475 degrees F. Place the eggplant and whole peppers on a sheet pan and coat with olive oil. Roast until the skins are blistered and charred, about 45 minutes. Set aside to cool.

Set a large sauté pan over medium heat and cover the bottom with olive oil. Add the onion and a sprinkle of salt, and cook until soft and beginning to caramelize and brown. Remove from the heat.

Peel the skin from the peppers and remove the seeds. Coarsely chop. Peel the skin from the eggplant and remove the big seed pockets. Coarsely chop. Add the peppers, eggplant, and onion to the bowl of a food processor and pulse to purée. Add the salt, sugar, and apple cider vinegar. Process until smooth, or leave it coarse, pulsing only 10 to 12 times. Taste for salt and adjust to your liking.

Prepare jars for canning. Add ajvar to the jars and gently tap the bottom of the jars on the counter to release any air bubbles. Using a damp clean towel, wipe the rims of the jars and place the lids and rings on the jars. Process in a water bath for 10 minutes, using half-pint or pint jars. Remove the jars with tongs and let them cool on the counter. When the ajvar is cool, remove the metal rings, check for proper seals, and label with date and contents. Store in a cool, dark cupboard until ready to use, for up to a year.

PANTRY NOTE: You can mix and match the peppers used in your ajvar. Hot peppers work well, but be careful to temper the heat with some sweet peppers to round out the taste. Once opened, store in the fridge, where it will keep for several weeks.

Hibiscus Peaches

[MAKES ABOUT 5 PINTS]

I started infusing fruit preserves with various herbs and spices as a way to lend a soft flavor and to maintain fruit color and integrity. The tropical flower hibiscus is available dried in most bulk sections of health-food stores. In Mexico people drink Agua di Jamaica, a refreshing pink beverage, and hibiscus is a fairly typical ingredient in tropical tea blends. I use hibiscus with peaches, both for its tart finish and its pink hue. It keeps the peaches from turning dingy in the jar, and the leftover canning liquid makes a stunning syrup when boiled down. For specific details on canning, follow the directions outlined in the "Water-Bath Canning 101" sidebar.

5 pounds peaches

SYRUP
6 ½ cups water
1 cup sugar
2 lemons, halved
3 tablespoons dried hibiscus

Prepare jars for canning.

Bring a large pot of water to a boil. Make an ice bath by filling a large bowl with cold water and several ice cubes. Lay a sheet pan next to the ice-water bath. Working in quick succession, drop the peaches into the boiling water for 1 minute. Scoop them up with a slotted spoon and immediately drop them into the ice bath to stop the cooking. Once cooled, move the peaches over to the sheet pan. Continue in this fashion until all the peaches have been processed, replenishing the ice cubes as needed.

Empty the ice-bath bowl and refill it with cold water. Add two lemon halves, first squeezing out the juice. Working quickly, one peach at a time, cut each peach in half. With a paring knife, peel the skin from the halves (it should come off easily) and remove the pits. Put the peach halves immediately into the cold lemon water so they don't brown from air exposure. Work in this way until all your peaches have been peeled.

In a large saucepan over medium-high heat, put 6 ½ cups of water, sugar, 2 lemon halves, and hibiscus leaves (loose) and bring to a low boil. Have your jars ready. Drain the peaches and add them to the hibiscus syrup, cooking for 5 minutes. Do not cook the peaches any longer than 5 minutes, or they will turn mushy and lose their shape.

Pack the jars, adding peaches until they reach the bottom ring on the top of the jar, being mindful not to press down on them. On a folded-over dish towel (for padding), strongly tap the bottom of the jar on the counter, to help pack down the peaches. Fill the jar once more, leaving ½ inch of headspace.

When the jars are full, using a ladle or a liquid measuring cup for ease, pour the hot hibiscus syrup over the peaches, leaving ½ inch of headspace. Using a chopstick or skewer, gently stir the peaches to release any air bubbles. Wipe the rims of the jars, using a damp clean towel, and put the lids and rings on the jars. Process in a water bath for 20 minutes if using pint jars, 25 minutes if using quart jars.

While the peaches are in the water bath, place any remaining peach liquid over high heat and reduce until thick, like syrup. Pour this syrup into small 4-ounce canning jars and process in the water bath as you did for the peaches.

Remove the jars with tongs and let them cool on the counter. When cooled, remove the metal rings, check for proper seals, and label with date and contents. Store in a cool, dark cupboard until ready to use, for up to a year.

PANTRY NOTE: You'll need 2 pints (or 1 quart) of peaches to fill a pie. Once opened, peaches will keep in the fridge for several weeks but may discolor, so it's best to use them within 2 weeks. Any leftover peach hibiscus syrup can be added to batidos or drizzled over pancakes or ice cream. Fruit syrups make lovely hostess gifts.

SCENTED SUGARS

Sugar picks up flavors easily and is therefore a great medium for infusing. A scented sugar is a subtle addition to items that are baked as well as to hot beverages, but it can also be a great flavor addition to ice cream and custards. Any perfumed and edible flower will work well—lavender, rose, or scented geranium, my favorite. Vanilla is also a common scented sugar no urban pantry should be without. Scented sugars are easy to make, and they store indefinitely. Store them in small glass jars in a dark, cool cupboard away from any heat source. It's important to make sure that your flowers and herbs are clean and completely dry before adding them to the sugar, or the moisture will cause the sugar to clump.

There are two techniques for scenting sugar. I use them both, depending on how much time I want to dedicate to a project. The simple version of infusing sugar requires layering an herb or flower with sugar. In this way, sugar is generally scented within two weeks but will hold indefinitely. For more immediate results, I pulverize leaves or flowers along with half the sugar called for. In this way, oils are released into the sugar and flavor it quickly.

Vanilla Sugar

[MAKES 2 CUPS]

I like to grind up my vanilla beans so the entire jar of sugar is flecked with little brown specks of vanilla bean hull. I love this sugar sprinkled over frothy milk on top of my morning coffee. It can be used in place of plain sugar in most baking recipes.

1 fresh vanilla bean, cut into 4 pieces
2 cups granulated sugar

Put the vanilla bean and half of the sugar in a blender and set to chop. The vanilla bean should break up fairly readily, although you may need to pause and give your machine a shake, so as not to powder the sugar and to rotate any whole, unbroken bean. When all pieces of the vanilla bean have been chopped to small bits, stir in the remaining sugar. Place the mixture in a glass jar and store in a cool, dark cupboard. Keeps indefinitely.

Anise Hyssop Sugar

[MAKES 1 CUP]

Anise hyssop is a licorice-scented herb that I grow and use liberally for its distinct flavor. In sugar the herb's minty qualities are nearly lost, but the gentle licorice shines through.

1 cup sugar
2 large anise hyssop leaves, torn into pieces
Anise hyssop petals, from 1 flower head (if in bloom)

In a small glass jar, add a few spoonfuls of sugar. Place one tear of an anise hyssop leaf, along with some petals on top, and then cover with another few spoonfuls of sugar. Continue in this fashion until all anise leaves, anise petals, and sugar are layered and used. Store the sugar in a cool, dark cupboard. Remove petals and leaves before using. Keeps indefinitely.

Rose Geranium Sugar

[MAKES 1 CUP]

Scented geraniums are a wonderful way to introduce floral notes to your cooking without need-ing to gather loads of petals. Geraniums come scented in many notes (see Scented Geraniums in chapter 9, "The Pantry Garden"), but my favorite for baking is rose geranium. It is perfect paired with such fruits as strawberries and rhubarb. Use it in place of plain sugar in ice cream and serve alongside a bowl of berries.

4 large fresh geranium leaves
1 cup sugar

Put 3 geranium leaves and half of the sugar in a blender and chop. The leaves will break up fairly read-ily, although you may need to pause and give your machine a shake, so as not to powder the sugar. When the leaves are finely chopped, pour the mixture into a fine-mesh strainer set over a small bowl. Shake the sugar over the bowl, straining out any large leaf bits. (You can compost the leaf bits.) Stir in the remaining sugar. Place in a small glass jar, layering the extra geranium leaf in the middle. Store in a cool, dark cupboard. Keeps indefinitely.

Fizzy Ginger Soda

[MAKES 1 GALLON]

When my brother and sister and I were feeling ill as youngsters, my mother always soothed our upset tummies with ginger ale. Over time I began to think of it as a miracle elixir. When I discovered you could make ginger soda at home, I started experimenting immediately. Fermentation is another form of preservation that many cultures have used for centuries. Sauerkraut, barrel pickles, corned beef, and kimchi are all great examples of fermented foods. Fermented foods take advantage of the natural process of converting sugar to alcohol (as with wine) or creating lactic acid (using bacteria to ferment foods, as in yogurt).

The ginger soda uses naturally occurring yeasts to ferment sugar into alcohol, which creates a light carbonation in the drink. Start to finish, this process takes about three weeks, possibly less time. The fermentation does create a small amount of alcohol in the final beverage, but not enough to get children loopy by any means.

START
1 cup water
2 teaspoons sugar
2 teaspoons ginger, freshly grated
Cheesecloth

SODA
8 cups water
One (2- to 3-inch) piece of ginger, grated
1½–2 cups sugar
3 limes, grated outer peel and juice
Water

Begin with the ginger start. Combine 1 cup water, 2 teaspoons sugar, and 2 teaspoons ginger in a small bowl and stir well. Cover the bowl with a piece of cheesecloth, folded into several layers. This will keep gnats and insects out but allow air in. Hold the cheesecloth in place with a tight rubber band and store the bowl in a warm spot in your kitchen. Every two days, add another 2 teaspoons sugar and

2 teaspoons ginger. Stir and cover with each addition, leaving the mixture to sit for a total of 8 days. After that, your start should be bubbly and fermenting. If not, continue adding sugar and ginger in equal proportions every 2 days, until bubbly and active.

Next make the soda. In a large saucepan, boil the water, ginger, and sugar. Once boiling, remove the mixture from the heat and stir in the grated lime peel. Set aside. Meanwhile, strain the liquid from your ginger start, passing through a cheesecloth until the liquid is fairly clean and clear. (Reserve the pulp from the ginger start—see Pantry Note below about restarting a batch of ginger soda.) Set aside the ginger start liquid. Once the soda water has completely cooled, strain out the ginger and lime peel. Add the lime juice and the ginger start liquid. Add water to this mixture until it measures 1 gallon.

Bottle in a sealable jar or a recycled plastic soda bottle (any container that is sealable will suffice). If using large (or small) bail-top jars or jugs with a rubber gasket, clamp down the gasket fully to seal. (I use two half-gallon wide-mouth mason jars.) If reusing plastic bottles, screw on the lid but leave a bit of give in the torque, so air is able to move about some. Store in a warm, dark spot for 10 to 14 days before opening. This allows time for fermentation to occur. Cool your jars before opening. Cooling halts the fermentation process. Be careful when opening, as carbonation has built up and soda may escape from the bottle quickly.

PANTRY NOTE: You can restart a batch of ginger soda by using the same start pulp you strained and adding 1 cup of water, 2 teaspoons of ginger, and 2 teaspoons of sugar. Also, if carbonation is very strong, it's possible that some bottles may explode during fermentation. Make sure to store in a cool place, away from other foodstuffs. I store my jars in my pots and pans cupboard. Craft-brewing supply stores carry 12-ounce "beer" bottles and caps, if you'd like to bottle your ginger soda individually.

Creative Infusions

An infusion is simply the process of steeping an ingredient (most often a plant) into a liquid solution to scent or flavor the liquid in some fashion. Most people are familiar with the concept: tea leaves are commonly infused into hot water for a cup of tea. Within the parameters of your pantry, however, infusions create an opportunity to put your creative stamp on a recipe.

Most liquids pick up the flavor from an infusion when slightly heated and then left to cool, as in Homemade Vanilla Ice Cream (in chapter 7, "Milk & Yogurt"), where the vanilla pod is left to sit in warmed milk for a length of time. When inventing your own infusion profiles, it helps to start thinking of recipes that contain a fair amount of liquid—anything with milk, water, vinegar, or oil as a main component. Vanilla Quinoa Pudding (in chapter 3, "Whole Grains") takes kindly to some kind of spicy perfume in the milk. Any ice cream recipe can be easily infused. Soups are great mediums for infusions, as are fried foods in which you can scent the oil. When I was young, my mother would add bacon fat to the shortening she used for frying chicken. She didn't note it as such, but she was essentially infusing the shortening with bacon. Mmmmm. Vinegar is another great medium for infusing. You can scent your pickles with lemon rind (see Indian Pickled Carrots in this chapter) or add some orange rind to your peaches (see Hibiscus Peaches in this chapter). You just have to get creative.

Infusions can be made of any plant—tea, spices, fresh herb, grain, and so on. I keep a few small muslin bags in my pantry for infusing. They are reusable, wash easily, and don't leave behind any linty residue as cheesecloth sometimes can when it's frayed. You can find muslin bags at most specialty kitchen or tea shops, or even at your grocery. Often, infusions are strained before adding the liquid to the final recipe, so these little bags come in quite handy, particularly when using a fine-textured ingredient like small-leafed teas.

When deciding which infusion to make, it's helpful to consider cultures and natural fits for food. Ginger, for instance, is a staple ingredient in Asia, so if I want to infuse a ginger-heavy recipe like the Fizzy Ginger Soda (in this chapter), I'll look to other typical Asian ingredients—chiles, cilantro, lemongrass, peanuts, coconut, and so on—and then narrow down what would work best. For the ginger soda, lemongrass and cilantro seem like a nice subtle complement. I haven't tried infusing the water for the soda yet, but I think I may now! Here are a few other options for infusions, in addition to my favorite dried fruit infusion (see Steeping Fruit in chapter 1, "Stocking the Pantry"). Experiment and come up with your own. I bet you'll find something you love, and if nothing else, you'll start thinking creatively about your food and writing your own recipes. Exciting stuff!

ginger soda + fresh lemongrass = lemongrass ginger soda

quinoa pudding + chamomile = chamomile vanilla pudding

simple sour cherries + vanilla bean = vanilla pie cherries

rhubarb + rose geranium sugar = rosy rhubarb jam

sage leaves + water + polenta = sage polenta

ice cream base + Earl Grey tea = Earl Grey ice cream

ice cream base + popped corn + salt = popcorn ice cream

stock + ginger + green onion = Asian soup broth

apple + star anise = spiced apple butter

brandy cherries + orange peel = brandied cherries with orange

Apple & Quince Butter

[MAKES ABOUT 5 HALF PINTS]

I can never decide which I like better—apple butter or quince butter—so I started using equal amounts in my butter recipes and the results are excellent. Quince is not widely available, so if you can't find it, double up on the apples. I live in apple country (Washington State) and seek out heirloom apples whenever I can. I prefer Winesap, but plenty of other varieties work well in this recipe: Empire, Macintosh, Rome, and Spitzenburg. Fruit butters sit on low heat for a very long time before thickening, so make sure to plan on a few hours for this recipe. For specific details on canning, follow the directions outlined in the "Water-Bath Canning 101" sidebar.

> 2 cups water
>
> 4 cups organic apple cider
>
> 2 pounds apples, scrubbed and chopped into 1-inch pieces
>
> 2 pounds quince, scrubbed, peeled, and chopped into 1-inch pieces
>
> 2 cups sugar
>
> 1 lemon, halved and juiced
>
> 1 teaspoon freshly ground cinnamon
>
> ½ teaspoon freshly ground clove
>
> ½ teaspoon freshly grated nutmeg

Put a small plate in the freezer (you will use this later to check the set). Put the water, apple cider, apples, and quince in a large stockpot. The liquid in the pot should just cover the fruit. If there is not enough liquid, add apple cider or water to cover. Place over medium to medium-high heat and bring to a simmer. Cook until all the fruit is soft and you can mash it with the back of a spoon.

Working in batches, put the fruit in a blender (only half full at a time, as hot liquids expand) and purée. (You may also use a food mill for this step, which will help strain out seeds.) When all of the fruit is puréed, put it back into the pot. Add the sugar, lemon juice and halves, cinnamon, clove, and nutmeg and return the mixture to medium heat.

Fruit butter takes a long while to thicken. Keep your stockpot over medium to medium-low heat, stirring continuously every few minutes, taking care not to let it burn. If the fruit butter is too hot and sticking to the bottom of your pot, adjust the heat down. The butter is done when a small spoonful is placed on a plate and no liquid separates out, creating a ring around the fruit butter. Cooking time can take anywhere from 1 hour to 2 hours. Remove lemon halves.

While the butter thickens, prepare jars for canning. You'll need to sterilize the empty jars for this recipe.

Add the thickened fruit butter to sterilized jars, and gently tap the bottom of the jars on the counter to release any air bubbles. Using a damp clean towel, wipe the rims of the jars, and place lids and rings on the jars. Process in a water bath for 5 minutes.

Remove the jars with tongs and let cool on the counter. When cooled, remove the metal rings, check for proper seals, and label with date and contents. Store in a cool, dark cupboard until ready to use, for up to a year.

PANTRY NOTE: Apple & Quince Butter is great on toast, of course, but it can be used in lots of clever ways. Smear a layer of fruit butter on puff pastry, cover with thinly sliced apples, sprinkle with demerara sugar, and bake for an easy dessert. Apple butter can also be used to line the base of a tart, such as the Almond–Butter Tart in chapter 6, "Nuts." Spread a thin layer on the bottom of the tart shell, add the nut–butter mixture and fruit filling, then bake as directed.

chapter 9

the pantry garden

IN MY LIFE OUTSIDE OF THE KITCHEN, I am a gardener. Not just any ol' gardener—I'm an urban gardener. I plant edible gardens for city folk in their backyards, frontyards, parking strips, and among various pots and containers. Anywhere I can find space, I tuck in edibles, both annuals and perennials, for people to grow and eat. Fruit trees, cane berries, artichokes, lettuces, tomatoes, cukes, and as many herbs as I can fit are squeezed into small urban lots to attract the eye and inspire people to cook. In an urban setting, you need to be resourceful if you're going to grow your own food.

Small kitchen gardens are an incomparable extension to a well-stocked pantry. Like a lot of urban dwellers, I live in an apartment in the heart of the city. I don't have a lawn, and I don't have pretty flower beds. My frontyard is made entirely from a row of Dumpsters and a large parking lot. One lone scraggly tree keeps sentry. What I lack in frontyard space I make up for in patio real estate on a decent-sized deck, where I keep container plants in the warmer months (or cold months if any plant is hardy enough to survive unattended). Over the years I have kept a container garden for edibles and narrowed down my choices to vegetables, herbs, and flowers that are prolific producers and add flavor to meals. Aside from the obvious natural beauty in a pantry garden, there is a beauty in the ability to experiment. I came into urban "farming" not because I have a bright-green thumb but because I love food. When the season is high, each day something can be clipped from the garden—an herb for garnish or flower petals for preserving. At home you can grow herbs and edibles that are not readily available in grocery stores or farmers markets. Growing your own herbs and food is like a gateway drug to a new world of flavors in your cooking. You'll become addicted.

Equally important are the sheer economics involved in growing food at home. A cluster of fresh herbs may cost three to five dollars at the grocery store, and it's rare that you'll use the entire package in a single recipe. One plant start costs about the same. Ditto for a package of seeds, which often contains twenty-five seeds or more. Seed swapping is truly the best deal of all. Sharing a packet of seeds among friends allows you to split the cost and sort through others' seed stocks for inspiration. Co-oping and bartering are natural extensions of the DIY (do-it-yourself) culture. The initial investment in pots, potting soil, and seeds works out in your favor with each continued year of growing. For renters, containers allow you to pack up your garden with you when you leave the property. It helps the budget to be resourceful when considering your growing container. Look for salvaged goods that can hold soil. I have used old wine crates (that I pulled from a trashbin), asparagus crates (that I take from a local restaurant each spring), and old tins and milk crates. Some of these are not the most cosmetically inspiring, but they cost nothing and hold soil well enough to grow in. Make a funky hodgepodge of used materials and you may wind up with a quaint little garden spot after all.

Being thrifty is at the heart of homegrown herbs, flowers, and food. Most plants allow you to clip only what you need, and often they'll fill in before you take to them again. Herbs are either perennial, meaning they come back each year, or annuals that will reseed. Last year was the first year that I only planted lettuces by hand. All my other herbs and flowers reseeded themselves on my deck without me having to think about it (and frankly before I had time to plan my home garden).

Although I am a huge fan of planting herbs and lettuces in container gardens, there are not many other edibles that grow as successfully or work out economically when grown in small pots ("small" being the operative word here). The economics of growing food at home take into account the duration of a plant's life cycle, the amount of space the plant needs to prosper, how much a single plant will produce, and how widely available that produce is in the marketplace. Yes, you can grow a tomato in a pot, but for the size of pot it requires, that prime container real estate is better suited to a plant that will continue putting out over the course of a season. For that reason, this chapter steers clear of covering all bases of container edibles; rather, I focus on growing plants that supply your urban pantry in a steady stream and don't take up much space. To plant in this fashion adds to the larder and should inspire you to use what's ripe and ready. Best of all, growing at home keeps you in tune with the season. Pretty soon, you'll notice slight differences in temperature and length of day. It's a happy consequence of pursuing homegrown goodness.

Many herbs in recipes can be swapped out with success. Start small and keep growing as you decide what you do and don't use from your garden. The pantry garden is one of life's little luxuries, so remember to water your plants regularly, experiment with a mix of starts and seeds, and get growing already!

HERBS & FLOWERS

Herbs are a no-brainer and something I use often in my cooking. Fresh herbs brighten up dishes, add an eye-pleasing punch of color, and in the best cases enhance the flavor of a dish in just the right way. Herbs accomplish what no other cooked ingredient can: adding life to a dish, literally. Certain herbs, however, are not necessarily the wisest to grow, given limited space. I count parsley, basil, and cilantro among them for several reasons. I tend to use a large amount of these herbs in my recipes. Think about homemade salsa—you can easily chop an entire bunch of cilantro for one recipe. Cutting this much from a homegrown container planting would wipe out the entire crop. Same goes for flat-leaf Italian parsley and basil. Because they are typically used in large quantities, it doesn't make sense to grow these herbs for an urban pantry. (Unless you have plenty of space in your yard, which is another concept entirely.) All of these herbs are readily available in fresh form in most groceries, and are typically much cheaper than others.

Anise Hyssop

Anise hyssop is my favorite herb. I am constantly growing it and thrusting it onto friends and neighbors. Every time I take a bite, I can't believe the flavor! Part licorice, part mint, a little bit like honey—it's herbal perfection that you can't buy commercially. That means you have to grow it! I use anise hyssop in grain salads, to scent sugars, and as a digestive tea after a big meal or between courses. The plant makes a gorgeous bouquet: it grows tall with long, vibrant purple flowers. Anise hyssop is a perennial that will come back year after year.

WHEN AND WHERE TO PLANT. Anise hyssop should be sown in spring. One seed packet is more than enough to fill one pot. The seeds are tiny and blow away easily, so take care when planting. They need only be pressed delicately into the soil. If sown in fall, the seeds will not germinate until spring. Anise hyssop likes full to partial sun and will tolerate indirect light.

POT SIZE. A medium-sized pot works well, but I prefer a deep one so the roots have room to stretch down and grow long. If you allow for a large pot, the stalks can grow to over two feet tall—a stunning addition to any container garden.

SEEDS VERSUS STARTS. It's likely you'll need to purchase anise hyssop seed online, as it is not a popular herb.

HOW TO HARVEST. Cut off an entire stalk as close to the main stem as possible. When the plant flowers, cut the entire main stem. It may regenerate growth.

HOW TO EAT. Anise hyssop dries well, but I prefer leaves fresh off the plant in salads. It adds a nice flavor to a simple herbal green salad and is equally fantastic in a room-temperature grain salad—be it barley, quinoa, or another whole grain. Anise hyssop can be steeped in milk as flavor for ice cream. The licorice scent shines through and is an interesting alternative to vanilla—delicious when you serve a scoop with a pie, tart, or cookie. When the plant flowers, you can strip the purple blossoms and sprinkle them on salads for a shocking pop of color.

Chamomile

Chamomile is a dainty little white flower that looks like a tiny daisy. Run your hand over a swath of chamomile and the scent perfumes the air as well as your fingertips. This plant lends a very subtle floral–sweet note to recipes. Chamomile comes in many varieties, but German chamomile is the common plant for teas and infusions. This plant is a self-seeding annual. If you are growing it in a garden bed and do not wish it to spread, be sure to dead-head the plant; that is, remove all the dead, dry flower heads that hold the seeds.

WHEN AND WHERE TO PLANT. Chamomile prefers full sun and can be planted in late spring, once temperatures have warmed and remain consistent.

POT SIZE. German chamomile grows low to the ground and spreads and has a shallow root system. You can get away with tucking this plant into a small pot—say 6 inches deep and at least that wide at the rim. The larger the pot, the larger the harvest will be.

SEEDS VERSUS STARTS. Chamomile is somewhat difficult to germinate, so purchase one start for each pot. The plant will fill in and spread.

HOW TO HARVEST. Pop fresh flower heads off of the plant for use in recipes.

HOW TO EAT. Chamomile can be picked and left to dry on a sheet pan for several days if you do not use it straightaway. Chamomile heads can be crumbled into recipes or left whole. To make teas, or to infuse preserves, place chamomile heads in a reusable cloth spice bag to steep. Add chamomile to hot cereal in the morning, by crumbling a flower head in and stirring.

Chervil

Chervil is the new dill. A self-seeding annual, chervil is one of the very first plants to pop out of the soil and signal spring's arrival. Chervil is a tender herb with a delicate stem and soft, feathery leaves. Its flavor is a cross between parsley and tarragon, but more subtle. Chervil will set flowers and go to seed once spring turns warm, so it's best to cut and use the herb regularly. In mild climates, a second crop of chervil will often re-seed and grow back in fall.

WHEN AND WHERE TO PLANT. Chervil can be planted early in spring, once the danger of frost has passed, but when temperatures are still cool. It prefers part sun—a space with afternoon shade is perfect.

POT SIZE. Chervil gives and gives and gives. No matter how much you cut from the plant, it fills in quickly and fully. A medium-sized pot is large enough to keep you happy with chervil production all spring. The pot should be at least 12 inches deep and 10 inches wide.

Urban Pantry Herbs:
Planting Recipe

The secret to a good patio garden lies in preparation. Make sure to choose big pots so your herbs have room to grow. An abundance of fresh herbs is an ultimate luxury for amending the pantry. You'll need 1 bag potting soil, 1 herb start or packet of seeds, and 2 to 3 tablespoons all-purpose organic fertilizer, such as fish bone meal or kelp.

Make sure you choose a pot with drainage holes. (For specific pot sizes for various herbs, see details under each herb, in this chapter.) If using a plant start, fill the pot halfway with potting soil. Do not use regular topsoil or dirt, as it is too heavy and will not drain properly. Sprinkle in the fertilizer, and dig in with a small rake or kitchen fork. Remove the plant start from the nursery pot and gently massage the soil to break up the root ball. Trim the roots so they hang no more than 4 inches from the base of the plant. Place the start over the pot and align the base of the plant flush with the lip of the pot. With one hand holding the start steady, use your free hand to add soil to the pot, covering the plant roots and filling the pot with potting soil up to the lip. Potting soil should be flush with the top of the pot. Do not press down too firmly on the soil. Water deeply and place outside.

If using seeds, fill the pot until potting soil is flush with the lip of the pot. Water the soil before planting seeds. Watering first ensures drainage so you won't dislodge any freshly planted seeds. Sprinkle in the fertilizer and dig it in with a small rake or kitchen fork. Press the seeds into the surface of the soil and cover very lightly with a handful of potting soil. Lightly water the surface and place outside, being careful to keep the seed bed slightly moist until the plant germinates. You will likely need to water once a day or use a spray bottle to moisten the surface until germination. Once the plant germinates, keep the soil moist but not wet. Do not let the container dry out fully between waterings, unless otherwise noted for specific herbs.

SEEDS VERSUS STARTS. Chervil germinates fairly well (if the soil is kept moist) and is not widely available in nurseries, so planting from seed works best.

HOW TO HARVEST. Cut the chervil stem close to the soil and use both the stem and the leaves in your recipes.

HOW TO EAT. Chervil is best eaten within a day of harvest and left raw, or added to a hot dish just before serving so you don't lose the soft flavor. It's an excellent pairing with fish, particularly smoked fish like salmon and trout. Chervil is a partner to eggs as well—be they hard-cooked and cold or cooked as an omelet. Try it in potato salads in place of dill.

Lovage

Lovage looks like parsley but tastes celery-like, although the flavor is much more pronounced. This perennial plant comes back year after year, even in container pots. You can use every last inch of the lovage plant in the kitchen—leaves, seeds, stalks, and even the roots. If you live in a small condo or apartment and don't have garden space, lovage is an excellent choice as just a leaf or two will add intense flavor to a recipe. You do not need a huge plant or repeated sowings to make use of this herb. If, however, you have garden space, you should plant this one in the ground. Its girth will take over a large area, but the excess seeds it produces can be harvested midsummer for the spice pantry and the plant's blossoms attract good pollinators to the garden.

WHEN AND WHERE TO PLANT. Like most herbs, lovage needs to be sown in spring. I keep it in a large pot on my deck, which produces two main stalks a year, plenty for embellishing meals. If you have garden space, be sure to leave room around the plant, which may reach up to 9 feet tall and spread outward of 5 feet wide.

POT SIZE. A deep pot is best, as lovage has a thick and large root system. Choose a pot at least 18 inches deep and 12 inches wide.

SEEDS VERSUS STARTS. Purchase one lovage start per container. It will fill out and multiply over the course of a season and come back the next spring. If planting by seed, sow in early spring, once the danger of frost has passed. You need only two to four seeds to produce a healthy plant. If all seeds germinate, thin to two healthy plants after four weeks.

HOW TO HARVEST. Cut young stalks and leaves from the plant, or for large quantities cut off an entire stalk as close to the main stem as possible.

HOW TO EAT. Lovage is best served fresh or with very little cooking time. Chiffonade the leaves for use as garnish and flavor to finish a dish, or tear them roughly and add to salads. Lovage and seafood go well together. Chop some leaves and serve them over steamed mussels or seared fish fillets. The seeds can be used in cooking as you would use a celery seed. When the stalks are thick and woody (typically in midsummer), you can cut them and use them as straws—a particularly delicious option when drinking a Bloody Mary.

Mint

Mint gets somewhat of a bad rap because it's considered a runner, meaning the plant sends out roots just under the soil surface and spreads quickly, often taking over. Personally I never think of a mint invasion as a problem, but rather as an excellent opportunity to create more recipes. Mint is also well-suited to a large container, where a small start will multiply easily. You can decide how best to plant it—in the ground or in a pot, given your space. There are many varieties of mint available, but for the pantry choose spearmint for cooking, cocktails, and garnish. Mint is a perennial, and pending a hard winter it will come back every year, even if left unattended.

WHEN AND WHERE TO PLANT. Plant mint in the spring through early summer or fall in most areas. Plant in full to partial sun and keep the soil moist. Mint does not like wet "feet," meaning you should be careful the soil drains well and doesn't leave the bottom of a container soggy after watering.

POT SIZE. For a continuous supply of mint, choose a pot at least 10 inches deep and 9 inches wide (a medium-sized pot).

SEEDS VERSUS STARTS. Purchase one mint start per container. It will fill out and multiply over the course of a season and come back the next spring.

HOW TO HARVEST. Cut entire stems from the plant, at their base, as close to the soil as possible.

HOW TO EAT. Mint is a refreshing garnish for grilled and roasted meat and vegetables. Chop it up fine and smash into butter and use over your veggies or meat. Roughly tear mint leaves and add them to your salads, or finely chop and float them on broth soups. Mint is best when eaten fresh and not cooked for long. Mint can be steeped in milk as a flavoring for custards or in boiling water as a stomach-soothing tea that aids in digestion.

Nigella

Nigella is more commonly known as love-in-a-mist and several plant species go by the name. For culinary use, choose nigella sativa—also known as black cumin or onion seed. (The love-in-a-mist species is not traditional for culinary uses.) Nigella produces a thin stem with wispy fronds, and flowers bloom light cornflower blue. Once the flowers die, seed pods are produced in thin-skinned paper-lanternlike seed pods that contain the nigella seeds. Some people use the dried pods in floral arrangements, but I prefer to eat them!

WHEN AND WHERE TO PLANT. Nigella should be directly sown in spring and can be successively grown through early summer. This plant likes sun, but doesn't need constant exposure. A spot with morning sun works well. Nigella is a self-seeding annual.

POT SIZE. For the splash of color and the production of seeds, I give nigella lots of room to grow. Choose a deep pot—at least 18 inches. Width of the pot is not as important, as nigella grows tall and does not spread.

SEEDS VERSUS STARTS. Nigella is best sown directly.

HOW TO HARVEST. Leave plants to flower and turn to seed pods. When the seed pods have dried and turned brown, pull off the heads and shake out the seeds. Compost the seed pods, but save the seed and store in a glass spice container in your spice cupboard.

HOW TO EAT. Nigella seeds have a very distinct flavor, tasting of a florally cumin and pepper blend. They are absolutely unique and unmistakable. The seeds from the pod are asymmetric and intensely black. Nigella is best used as garnish on dishes or as an herbal infusion (detailed in chapter 8, "Small-Batch Preserving"). Sprinkle over Walnut & Garlic Chicken (in chapter 6, "Nuts"), add to a plate of beets, or garnish your morning eggs with these pretty seeds.

Sage

Sage is the ultimate winter herb, as it's an evergreen perennial. Although it is a fairly resilient plant, sage does have a tendency to get leggy and unsightly. It's best when pruned back in early spring, just before the plant will put on new growth. Sage comes in various scents (like tangerine sage or pineapple sage) and colors (variegated or purple-tinged leaves), lending itself well to adding variety to your pantry garden as well as new flavors to your meals.

WHEN AND WHERE TO PLANT. Sage seeds can be planted in mid-spring, once the ground has started to warm up a bit, although they can be difficult to germinate. Plant sage starts in mid- to late spring and keep them watered until established but not too wet, which could lead to rot. Sage is prolific in hot, dry climates, so it's best in full sun.

POT SIZE. A little sage goes a long way, so use a medium-sized pot for this herb. A 10-inch diameter and 12-inch depth should be enough to keep you in sage all year, needing to supplement only if you have a recipe calling for large quantities.

SEEDS VERSUS STARTS. Sage can be sown directly into a pot or a garden bed. Better still, it takes well to propagation, so you need only find a plant in spring, cut a portion from a stem tip, and stick it in a small pot. Keep moist but well drained until the sage starts developing roots, and then transplant to a larger pot.

HOW TO HARVEST. Cut whole sprigs from the main branch. Sage branches that have been stripped of leaves can be used to flavor stocks, or tossed onto a charcoal grill to lend some herbaceous flavor to the smoke.

HOW TO EAT. Sage adds flavor to all those hearty dishes associated with the cold months: stews, braises, roasted meats. Sage ice cream with huckleberry sauce is a mind-blowing dessert. Try it. Fruit-scented sages are fantastic torn and served with melon in summer or muddled in some boiling water for teas.

Herb Vinegar

Fresh herbs can get expensive if you're buying them at the store, so I like to grow my own. I always make sure to use every last sprig. If you have leftover herbs, or a prolific plant that needs cutting back, you can dry herbs for your spice cupboard (see the sidebar "Spice Cupboard" in chapter 6, "Nuts") or use them to flavor vinegar. Herb vinegars are made of two simple ingredients—vinegar and fresh herbs—and can be made in minutes. Subtle in flavor, herb vinegars impart an undertone of herb along with the tang of vinegar. They can be used in salads and vinaigrettes.

Use fresh healthy sprigs and distilled white vinegar for the best results. Any herb can work—try mint, lemon balm, basil, or tarragon. Use two sprigs of herb for every cup of vinegar. Add the sprigs directly to prepared jars. Use glass containers that can be sealed with a lid or cork. (Wash and sterilize jars for 10 minutes in a hot water bath before using.) Heat the vinegar until just beginning to boil and pour over the herbs, leaving a bit of head space. Store the vinegar in a cool, dark place for three to four weeks, checking the flavor after two weeks. When the flavor is to your liking, strain and discard the herbs and store the infused vinegar in a cool, dark cupboard.

Herb vinegars will keep for three months, longer if refrigerated. Be mindful of any mold or fermentation bubbles—this means the batch is spoiled and should be thrown out. As vinegar has a high acid content, there is no risk of botulism; mold and yeast are the two culprits of spoilage.

Scented Geraniums

I fell in love with scented geraniums early on in my gardening experimentation because they are nearly impossible to kill. They come back each year and survive with blatant neglect. Some varieties have variegated leaves, and many flower in varying shades of pink and white, but it's the foliage that holds the oil. To decide which geranium to purchase, rub a leaf gently between your thumb and pointer finger to pick up some of the plant's natural oil and smell it to see if you like the scent. Scented geraniums come in a wide range of "flavors"—mint, nutmeg, rose, lemon, and many others.

WHEN AND WHERE TO PLANT. Geraniums do well in dappled sun or partly shady spaces, so long as you have some sunlight. They can be planted nearly any time of the year. If you have winters with long freezes, move the plants inside until spring.

POT SIZE. You can use smaller pots for geraniums, as you don't need much for the pantry. A few leaves a year will keep you well-stocked. Choose a pot at least 8 inches deep. If you would like the plant to grow larger next year, transplant it to a bigger pot in the fall.

SEEDS VERSUS STARTS. You should purchase scented geranium starts. All geraniums may be propagated and make very special hostess gifts. (See note on propagation under "Sage.")

HOW TO HARVEST. Most plants do best when you harvest whole stems. In the case of scented geraniums, however, a little goes a long way so I sometimes choose big juicy leaves and pluck them from the main stem of the plant. If using several leaves, cut an entire stem from the plant.

HOW TO EAT. While I fell in love with scented geraniums for their ease of growing, it wasn't until later that I realized the leaves could be used to scent desserts and sugars. Scented geranium leaves can be steeped in milk for floral-scented ice creams and custards. Steep some rose-scented leaves in warmed heavy cream, cool the cream back down, and then whip it into soft peaks of whipped cream and serve it with strawberries. All berries pair well with scented geraniums. The leaves can also be stored in sugar so it becomes infused (see Scented Sugars in chapter 8, "Small-Batch Preserving"), or left whole and crystallized in sugar for a pretty garnish.

Thyme

Thyme is one of the easiest most hassle-free herbs to grow. I planted some thyme seeds five years ago in a big terra-cotta pot, and every year it comes back to produce delicious fresh leaves. Most everyone thinks about thyme for stocks or roasting meats, but it can also be used in sweet desserts and pairs well with fruit such as plums and blueberries. Be sure when you purchase starts or seeds that you are selecting a culinary thyme, as there are many members in the thyme family and not all taste great. Lemon thyme has a distinctive citrus aroma and can be used in most recipes that call for English thyme.

WHEN AND WHERE TO PLANT. Thyme is a hardy herb and therefore adaptable to various weather conditions. Plant in spring, summer, or fall with good results. Thyme is sympathetic to shade, so it does not need full sun to be vigorous.

POT SIZE. Thyme has a shallow root system but will spread if you give it enough space. Opt to grow thyme in a wide shallow pot or even a wooden flat or box.

SEEDS VERSUS STARTS. Thyme is widely available as a start, but it also grows easily from seed.

HOW TO HARVEST. Choose whole branches of thyme and cut them at the base. You should also cut back your thyme in early summer after it blooms (June) so that it'll fill in and provide tender bushy growth all summer and through fall.

HOW TO EAT. Thyme is fantastic when used as a final garnish on savory tarts (see Onion–Thyme Tart in chapter 2, "Kitchen Economy"). Thyme goes hand-in-hand with a flavorful stock and an herby roast lemon chicken. Using that same flavor theme, thyme can be used in nearly all lemon desserts. It is best when cooked slightly, and dries very well for your spice cupboard.

LETTUCES

Lettuces are a very smart "crop" to grow at home. Farmers-market and store-bought lettuce sells for two to three dollars a head, or eight dollars a pound when loose. For eight dollars, you can purchase three varieties of seed that will keep you in lettuce nine months of the year.

Many lettuces grow to full heads in forty to sixty days, so I opt for a smattering of maturing times, which ensures that as one is finishing, another is just coming in. As lettuces have a shallow root system, they can be grown in the smallest of pots and don't take up much space. Lettuce can be harvested over the course of several months by trimming off only the outer leaves of the plant. They quickly fill back in. I use my lettuce for salads, as greens on sandwiches, and even as a fresh herb in a pinch.

Growing lettuce at home is made all the more appealing by the vast selection available from seed. Lettuce seeds come in a range of shapes, sizes, colors, flavors, and textures. Some are sweet, some are frilly, some are bitter, and some are speckled. Order a variety you've never heard of and give it a go. You'll likely be pleased with the surprise.

Look through any seed catalog and plan to mix soft, crispy, sweet, and bitter on one juicy fork-ful. Forellenschluss (heirloom speckled romaine), Lollo Rosso (frizzy red looseleaf), and Buttercrunch (green Bibb) are great choices for variety.

WHEN AND WHERE TO PLANT. Lettuces can be sown in early spring and throughout summer and fall. Frequent sowings guarantee a constant supply. Lettuce needs sun but can do with as little as six hours of direct sunlight a day. Sow 6 inches apart to allow room for heads to develop. You'll need to thin any lettuces that grow too close, so that one plant can come to maturity. Thinning is a natural process, and you actually do more damage by leaving plants to grow too close together than you do by removing one early on.

POT SIZE. After years of experimenting, I have found the perfect lettuce pot to be long, narrow, and shallow. Both terra-cotta and plastic pots come in this size, and they fit well butted up against the edges of a deck or tied to a railing or window sill. Make sure the soil depth is 6 to 8 inches. The pot need only be 4 inches wide. Get the length of pot that works best in your space. For me, the longer, the better to fit more lettuces in.

SEEDS VERSUS STARTS. Direct-sow lettuce from seed. Lettuce starts are one of the least economical vegetable starts to purchase. Buy seeds from a local organic resource when you can, or join a reputable seed swap like www.seedsavers.org. Some of my favorite resources for dependable and diverse seed are www.seedsofchange.com, www.rareseeds.com, and, for information only, www.organicseedalliance.org.

HOW TO HARVEST. As the plants grow, snap off the large outer leaves at the stem. The lettuce will fill in and continue producing leaves. Loose lettuces may be cut at the base of the stem when they reach 3 to 4 inches tall (for baby lettuce mix). If you leave your lettuces unharvested for too long, they'll often turn bitter in the heat. If this happens, harvest the entire head and hold it in a damp paper towel in your fridge crisper for two days. The leaves should sweeten up. A good rule of thumb (as with any grown vegetable) is to taste it! If you like the flavor, it is ready to harvest. There are no rights or wrongs when your personal taste is in question.

HOW TO EAT. Lettuces are the ultimate salad ingredient, particularly when it's hot in summer and you're craving light meals. Serve them straight out of the garden. Dress lettuces simply with olive oil and lemon juice, salt and pepper. Bitter lettuces may be treated like radicchio and tossed in some olive oil and grilled; this is a great addition to Panzanella Salad with Pickled Red Onions (in chapter 2, "Kitchen Economy") or when combined with fresh leaves and tomatoes. I have tasted lettuce soup before and liked it well enough. Replace spinach with lettuce in a soup recipe and see if you're happy with the results.

INDEX

173

about the author

Food enthusiast AMY PENNINGTON is the creator and owner of GoGo Green Garden, an edible gardening business that builds, plants, and tends edible gardens for city folk in their backyards. In 2009 Amy launched UrbanGardenShare.org, a garden website that pairs city gardeners with unused garden space via an online matching program.

Amy has been featured on *Martha Stewart Living Radio* and in national and international publications including *Sunset* magazine and the *Toronto Star*. She is a regular contributing writer to *Edible Seattle*, a bimonthly food-focused magazine highlighting the culinary bounty of the Puget Sound region, and a guest contributor on the weekly radio program *In the Kitchen with Tom & Thierry*. She lives in Seattle. Visit www.gogogreengarden.com to learn more.

about the photographer

Della Chen is a documentary photographer who likes to eat, travel, and shoot. Visit www.dellachen.com.